222 Ways to
Entrepreneurial Success
By Brendan McGinty and Sherry Schuller

222 Ways to Entrepreneurial Success
Brendan McGinty and Sherry Schuller

Published by Leo Media, Inc.
1808 Woodfield Dr., Suite 203
Savoy, IL 61874-9440
(800) 421-6999

Find us on the World Wide Web at http://www.leomedia.net

Editor: Vanessa J. Krulas
Printing History: February 2004, First Edition

ISBN 0-9748941-0-9

Printed and bound in the United States of America

*To my late grandfather, Glenn Poor, Sr., a lifelong entrepreneur
whose legacy has continued for over 50 years and counting.
- BMM*

*To my mentor, my confidant, my best friend –
who has taught me there's really
only one secret to success.
- SLS*

Acknowledgements

We would like to thank Vanessa J. Krulas and Michael A. Hall for their help with editing and reviewing this book.

Table of Contents

Introduction

Our goal for this book is to bridge the information gap between knowing what it takes to start a business and being a successful entrepreneur.

We are not providing all answers to all business questions. Rather, we are helping to provide a foundation for entrepreneurs to be successful as well as encouragement to think creatively about ways in which you can differentiate yourself from your competition.

If you are thinking about starting a business, this book will help you to take the first steps to implementing your ideas and help you to gain an understanding of the various aspects of business. Through example case studies and short, powerful tips covering such entrepreneurial activities as corporate formation, early stage financing, legal and accounting guidance, and marketing and advertising, this book identifies the key factors that contribute to the growth of your organization.

If you're already in business, many of the tips contained in this book will help to solidify how you run your business and provide a creative source for growth strategies. There may be instances when you already know about the topic but need a refresher, or there may be issues you simply haven't considered, perhaps because your business or the times are changing. Use the book as a reference guide - easy reading only requiring a few minutes here and there to keep the important topics contained herein in the forefront of your mind, or spur brainstorming and creative thinking on ways in which you can further grow your success.

To all of you embarking on or continuing the journey of entrepreneurial success, we hope you enjoy this book and wish you all of the best.

Brendan McGinty

Sherry Schuller

Start-Up

If you want to make an apple pie from scratch,
you must first create
the universe.
Carl Sagan

#1 Things to Consider Before Starting a Business

You've got an idea or a desire to be an entrepreneur, a business owner. But have you considered everything before jumping in with both feet? Before you incorporate and write a business plan you should consider a few things.

Are you ready to dedicate the time and resources required to start a small business? Starting your own business often means running the show on your own before you can afford to bring on any assistance.

Are you starting your own business for the right reasons? If you're thinking of owning your own business because you're unhappy with your current job or you've just been laid off, this might not be enough reasoning for starting your own business. You need to make sure you're doing it because it's something you want to do – not because it's something you think you have to do or because you feel like it's your only option.

Are you financially ready to start up your own business? There are numerous ways entrepreneurs can obtain funds for starting a business, but most financiers will still expect you to invest some of your own money to show that you are risking something other than your time because you believe in your own ability and in your business. Expect to spend money and expect to not pay yourself for the good of the company.

There are several other things you'll want to ask yourself before you launch your business. Does your personality and people skills mesh well with an entrepreneurial lifestyle? Will you have the support of family and friends? Is there a market for your product or service? Who is your competition? What is your competitive advantage? There are plenty of things to consider. Just be sure that you've thought it all through so you don't end up surprising yourself after you've already committed to making it happen.

#2 Five Tips for Starting a Business

1. Before starting up your own business ask yourself
    what reasons you have for wanting to run your own
    show. Knowing why you want to be a business
    owner will help you to determine what kind of
    business is right for you. Once you know why
    you're in it and what you're in for, look to the
    experts for help with a business plan. It's the start
    of all that's to come.

2. If your business requires equipment to run,
    consider starting with used or lower-end equipment
    until your revenue increases and you can afford to
    upgrade. Look to the local classifieds or eBay for
    interim supplies.

3. As a new business, one of the easiest ways to get
    noticed and start a clientele is to be different and
    stand out. Creativity will differentiate you from your
    competition as well as gain you recognition and
    consumer awareness. Look to Seth Godin's book
    titled *Purple Cow: Transform Your Business by
    Being Remarkable* for inspiration.

4. Start small – that's why they call it a small
    business. Don't spend all of your money right from
    the start setting up your business. Spend your
    funds on developing and marketing revenue-
    generating products or services. You can use your
    profits to fund the rest. If you can't afford to market
    your new business, find bartering opportunities to
    promote your new business. Save costs by starting
    small from your home office, using what supplies
    you have on-hand before you buy.

5. Get assistance. There are plenty of free resources and help out there for you. Why pass it up? Look to your local economic development organizations, small business development centers, Service Corps of Retired Executives (SCORE), and the Small Business Administration (SBA) for information on low-cost or free classes for entrepreneurs and other great resources that will help you to make the best decisions for your business.

#3 Determining if there's a Market for Your Business

A Sure Entrepreneur

It seems like a simple question: is there a market for my business? Unfortunately, in the haste to form a company or expand upon an idea, many people starting businesses without taking the time necessary to determine if their company even has a chance at success.

Ask that question and do the necessary analysis. Analyze if your company has a market – if people will pay for what you plan to offer, whether it's a product or a service. Analyze the competition relative to your place in the market, both in terms of uniqueness and geographic proximity. Determine how much is spent in your market and conservatively estimate how much of that market you can get by implementing your business plan.

If you determine that there is no market for your business, save yourself the trouble and potential heartache and don't continue. Establish a business with a clear market; something where your expertise lends itself toward getting a piece of the market that is worth it to you.

#4 Start-up Costs to Consider

When you're planning on how you'll use your funds be sure to consider all of the costs associated with starting and growing your business. These include:

- *Legal costs*
  There will be costs associated with registering your business, structuring your business, and registering trademarks, patents, and copyrights. You may also wish to have an attorney review contracts you create including employee contracts, corporate employee handbooks, vendor agreements, or other business documentation.

- *Stationery, logos, letterhead*
  Branding your business right from the start will make marketing efforts easy. Consult with a marketing and advertising firm to have a professional logo designed for your company. Carry that logo over to all of your marketing material including stationery, letterhead, and other materials you intend to give out to prospective clients and partners.

- *Sales literature*
  Sales literature can include brochures, catalogs, business cards, fliers, and other materials used by your sales team to promote your products or services. Also, it's a good idea to include your marketing and advertising firm in the design of this material to promote a consistent message to your prospects.

- *Fixing up store/office*
  Inevitably, there will be costs associated with fixing up your office or store and making it presentable to prospective clients. This "package" is as important as your sales literature and is often one of the first impressions made on your prospects. Invest in the appearance of your business' environment.

- *Computer/Equipment expenses*
  From merchant accounts to fax machines, there are numerous expenses you will incur when first purchasing or leasing computers and other equipment necessary to doing business. Prioritize your list based on each item's involvement in your ability to sell your product or service to your clients. A fax machine may be a valuable investment, but if most of your orders come from walk-in visitors, it would probably be wiser to invest in your storefront.

  Also, consider leasing equipment as an alternative to purchasing. It will help string out your funds and provide you with more capital to get sales going before incurring large expenses.

Of course, these are only a few of the many expenses you'll incur as a growing business. Other expenses may include rent before start-up, insurance, salaries, and other costs associated with initially getting your business going.

#5 How Much Money do you need for a Start-up?

Starting a company has many factors in establishing success. Do you have a unique idea? Can you sell it? Do you have the resources to succeed? One of the most important resources you'll need is money.

Most small businesses suffer from a lack of sufficient financing. You need money to make money, and sometimes that's going to take giving up a piece (percentage) of your business to get the funds necessary for success. In fact, when you ask for money from an angel investor or venture capitalist, many times they'll ask the important question, "is that enough?" when it comes to your request for funds.

Determine how much money you'll need to do it right, to implement your business plan in as close to the ideal environment as possible. You may have to ratchet your request down depending on the availability of funds, but plan for success, and that includes asking for enough money. It's then up to you to justify your request and subsequent use of those funds.

#6 Business Legal Structures

The legal structure of your company is important because it can protect you legally as well as save you money in taxes. The legal structure of your company can change over time as your company changes as well.

If you're a one-person shop, most people form a sole proprietorship. Early stage companies that may take a year or more to start making money form a subchapter-S corporation. Partnerships may choose to form a Limited Liability Partnership (LLP) or Limited Liability Corporation (LLC). Mature established companies are many times a C-corporation.

The importance of finding a good corporate attorney cannot be underestimated. They will help you determine which corporate structure fits your needs, and will work with you as needs change.

#7 Advantages of Incorporating

Incorporating is a good way to keep your business and personal financial lives separate, protecting each from things that could adversely affect you personally or professionally.

There are different types of corporations – subchapter S, C, limited liability – that protect you in different ways depending on your structure. For example, Limited Liability Corporations (LLC) or Partnerships (LLP) are good for businesses with partners. Subchapter S corporations are good for young companies investing in their future and not likely to see profitability for a year or two because a percentage of losses can be applied to personal finances.

Read up on-line about the differences or consult a good corporate attorney. The right kind of formation for your company is important to its success.

#8 Best Ways to Incorporate

First determine what kind of corporate formation you want or need – subchapter S, C, LLC, LLP, or sole proprietorship. While it is possible to complete incorporation on-line, it's best to work with a corporate attorney you are comfortable with to ensure that the corporation is set up per your specifications.

Once incorporated, that same relationship with your attorney will help you work through the ongoing requirements for keeping your business incorporated. Many states require annual registration for your business, and a good corporate attorney will know all of the rules and regulations.

#9 Write an Effective Business Plan

When you have a business idea or as your existing business changes, you should write or update your business plan. The business plan guides your company, providing structure around your ideas and goals.

An ineffective business plan will prevent you from getting funding. There are many guides for writing an effective business plan. The Small Business Administration (SBA) has both guidelines for writing business plans as well as volunteer retired executives who can advise you on your business plan.

Check out the SBA web site at www.sba.gov for more information on writing business plans.

#10 Choose a Business Location

Depending on the type of business you have, the location of your business may or may not be important. Certainly, if you are in retail sales, location can be much more important than if you are in a nonproduct-based business.

For retail businesses, street level location, handicap accessibility, traffic density, and proximity to other successful retail businesses can all play a key role in the success of your business. The old adage can be true that "location is everything."

In non-retail businesses, sometimes the type of space (square footage, warehouse availability, number of private offices, etc.) is more important than location. Less populated areas may allow you to pay less per square foot. Again, your particular needs dictate your ideal location.

#11 Juggling Your Start-up and a Full-time Job

The Classic Juggler

In certain situations, you may be trying to get a start-up off the ground while still holding down a full-time job. Managing these two can be tricky because you don't want to not give your start-up enough attention, and you don't want to slight your full-time job at the same time.

If you want to do it right, expect long hours and less sleep. There's no other way around it. If you're committed to your start-up and loyal to your full-time job, expect to leave at some point but do so gracefully.

Don't lessen your performance at your full-time job. Do your start-up in your extra time, including on weekends, or get extra help to reach the goals you've set for your start-up. It might mean that your start-up takes a while longer to get rolling, but you almost always have time. Don't burn bridges at your full-time job. They may later be one of your clients.

Research

It is no longer our resources that limit our decisions; it's our decisions that limit our resources.
U. Thant

#12 Conducting Low-cost Market Research

If you're not familiar with some of the available research resources, market research can be costly. But there are plenty of ways you can research your market without incurring expenses.

When you're thinking of launching a new product, extend your market share, or find a new market for your existing product or service, look for secondary research first. This is research that others have already conducted and spent time and resources gathering. Why start from scratch if you can find credible information to start?

You should also start by attending industry events, such as conferences or trade shows, and listen to speakers or conversations between attendees. You can learn a lot from those in your industry.

You can also learn a lot from your customers, employees, prospects, and vendors. Just ask.

If you don't have the time or resources available to conduct your own market research, rather than incur the full costs of hiring a firm, consider partnering with a like company (not a competitor) and split the expense of the research.

#13 Use Census Data to Understand Your Market

If you're just getting started with your business or you can't afford to invest much money in researching your industry or market, try looking to the U.S. Census Bureau for valuable data that can help with making decisions or act as supportive documentation for your business' plan.

Census data includes information about population and businesses organized by state and county. You can study your industry using economic census data, learn about business markets and industry distribution, and analyze your prospective customers with the data provided by the Census of Population and Housing.

The best part is that nearly all census data is available for free via the Internet. Visit the U.S. Census Bureau's web site at www.census.gov for more information.

#14 Demographic & Psychographic Data
While researching your industry and your advertising targeted audience, it's a good idea to categorize the information you gather about your prospective clients and how they prefer to be serviced. Two of the most common ways of segmenting your data are demographic and psychographic profiling.

As it relates to your target audience, demographic data is statistical information about your audience's socioeconomic factors such as age, gender, income, occupation, education, etc. Advertisers will most likely provide you with demographic information about their audience. This is how you are able to match the demographics of your advertising audience with those of your prospective clients.

Psychographic data refers to information about your audience's lifestyle such as activities, interests, and opinions. This kind of data provides you with an understandable portrait of your customers and can be used to match your marketing venues with the lifestyle of your prospects.

Whether you choose to use both of these methods or just one, it's important that you take the time to research your prospects to find the most successful advertising venue – the one that targets the same audience.

#15 Researching On-line
Researching companies has been increasingly easier with the growth of the World Wide Web. If you're looking for information about businesses or prospective employees, consider the Internet your greatest resource. Here are some of the most useful sites for corporate research:

- *Hoover's On-line* – *www.hoovers.com*
  Look up industries, markets, and businesses by
  company name, ticker, industry keyword, executive
  name, and other search criteria.

- *Corporate Information* –
  www.corporateinformation.com
  International and U.S. company information
  including profiles, analyst reports, and earnings.

- *Search Systems* –*www.searchsystems.net*
  Free searchable public record databases for
  nationwide, state by state, territories, and
  worldwide.

- *Map Quest* – *www.mapquest.com*
  Looking for a map to your next meeting? Find the
  location, get directions, and arrive there with ease.

- *SuperPages* – *www.superpages.com*
  With over 16 million business listings nationwide,
  you're sure to find contact information in
  SuperPages' listings brought to you by Verizon.

- *Better Business Bureau* – *www.bbb.org*
  BBB reports provide information on over 2 million
  organizations. Do your research before getting
  involved!

- *D&B* – *www.dnb.com*
  Research a company, and purchase
  comprehensive reports that will help you to
  evaluate a company's financial stability, risk
  assessment, or risk of doing business with the
  company.

#16 Accessing D&B Information On-line

D&B stands for "Dun and Bradstreet" – one of the world's
leading providers of business information used by
customers who want to make purchasing decisions with

confidence. Similar to the Better Business Bureau, D&B provides information about businesses to consumers who are choosing a credible vendor or supplier or service provider.

As a consumer you can search companies by company name or by a D&B D-U-N-S number – a unique nine-digit sequence used to identify and keep track of more than 70 million businesses worldwide.

As a small business owner, a D-U-N-S number can enhance your credibility, increase awareness of your business' products and services, and provide you with an opportunity to work with the U.S. government and major businesses that require you to have a D-U-N-S number.

More information about Dun and Bradstreet is available at www.d&b.com.

#17 The Better Business Bureau
Similar to the Dun & Bradstreet organization, the Better Business Bureau (BBB) provides reports on over two million organizations. Consumers often use these reports to investigate organizations prior to doing business or investing.

As a consumer, you can view information about an organization, including any complaints filed against it, or file a complaint at www.bbb.org.

As an organization, you can build your business' credibility through joining a local Better Business Bureau.

#18 Subscribing to Magazines and Newspapers for PR Opportunities
If you've read any magazines or newspapers related to your industry lately you know that business owners wrote many of the featured articles. Subscribing to these publications will not only help you keep abreast of the news and trends in your industry, but it will also give you

opportunities for public relations such as writing your own article.

Look for unspoken advice or helpful information you can share with the publications' readers. Contact the publication's editors and ask for an editorial calendar. This will give you an idea of what's up and coming. The best way to get published is to write a feature related to the topics covered by the editorial calendar.

When you submit your article, include relevant photographs and mention its relation to the topic listed in the editorial calendar. Just be sure to submit well in advance of the publication's date!

#19 Your Competitors' Advertisements
One of the best ways you can learn about your industry and your prospective clients is to research your competitor's advertisements. This will not only give you insight regarding what you're up against, but it will also provide you with valuable information about the types of products and services that are being presented to your prospective clients.

Subscribe to industry magazines and newsletters and attend trade shows and expositions specifically designed for your clients. Study the advertisements your competitors have placed. Look for a need that isn't being offered, or a benefit that isn't being promoted, or better yet an audience that isn't being targeted!

You can learn a lot about your competitors by the size and frequency of the ads that they place. The bigger the ad or longer it's placed, the more likely they are to be raking in the revenue. Advertising costs businesses money. It also *makes* businesses money.

#20 Surveying Your Clientele
Conduct a customer survey or poll to be used on your web site, or include a reply card with invoices that you send to

your clients. Learn what they appreciate about your offerings and where they think you could improve upon your service or product.

Make sure you've made it as easy as possible for your clients to send you feedback. This means you'll want to keep the survey short and respect their time, as well as making it easy for them to submit the information to you. Consider including a self-addressed stamped envelope for your clients to return the survey if you're sending it by postal mail.

#21 Researching Your Customer Base
Your current clients are your most valuable assets. As a rule of thumb, it costs twice as much to attract a new client as it does to keep an existing one so take the time to research your customer base and learn everything about them that you can.

Classify and group your existing clients by common characteristics such as geographic location, age, gender, or other demographics. Then, find out why they work with you, how they found you, and what they like or don't like about your services or products. Surveying your customers will provide you with information that is key to growing your clientele and your business. You will learn their motivations for buying and be able to market your products and services based on these motivating factors.

You can also create focus groups to evaluate new products prior to developing and launching a full-blown marketing effort. This will help you to identify whether or not there is a need in your market for the product or service before investing resources.

If you don't already have customers, you can purchase mailing lists of prospective customers who match your target audience and survey these individuals or survey your competitors' clients if you're able to identify them. Don't forget to offer something to survey participants when

17

you ask for their time – the response rate will be greatly increased!

#22 Five Inexpensive Ways to Conduct Market Research

1. Survey your clients, prospects, partners, vendors, and suppliers.

2. Create a suggestion box.

3. Enclose questionnaires or business reply cards with every outgoing piece of mail.

4. Provide a "feedback form" on your business' web site.

5. Gather census data and demographics for your company's service area.

Product Development

If you can dream it, you can do it.
Walt Disney

#23 Offer a Modified Version of an Existing Product

One of the less expensive ways to increase your business' offerings is to look at your existing products and services and see if there is an opportunity to provide a modified version to your customers. If you're selling software, there may be an opportunity to sell a "lite" version of a full version product. If you're selling complementary products or services, consider bundling them together as a package.

You've already found consumers to purchase your existing products. Offering them modified versions makes marketing easy and affordable.

#24 Have Your New Product Evaluated Before Patenting

You have a great new idea. You've never heard of anything like it before. You want to protect your idea by writing and submitting a patent application. It's going to cost you a good chunk of money.

Before going to all of this trouble, consider having peers or others evaluate your product. This feedback could be and almost always is invaluable, as others typically think of an angle that you had yet to consider. Taking this extra time to set up trusted professionals to evaluate your product could save you from going down the wrong road, or could help to strengthen your patent application.

#25 What Is a UPC Code?

Are you planning to be in the business of selling products? If so, you'll need to invest in a Universal Product Code (UPC).

Just about every package you'll find has a UPC bar code printed on it. These 12-digit bar codes are used to identify products and information about your business. Some bar code numbers may be shortened if there are four consecutive zeros in the number, in which case they may be removed.

The number represented by the bar code is referred to as a Global Trade Item Number (GTIN) and is used to track sales and product orders by retail businesses internationally. A UPC Code allows you to track your products and product sales globally.

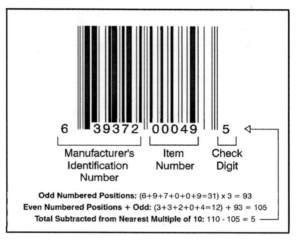

Manufacturer's Identification Number | Item Number | Check Digit

Odd Numbered Positions: (6+9+7+0+0+9=31) x 3 = 93
Even Numbered Positions + Odd: (3+3+2+0+4=12) + 93 = 105
Total Subtracted from Nearest Multiple of 10: 110 - 105 = 5

UPC Bar Code Anatomy

The first six digits of the code are referred to as the manufacturer identification number, with the first digit being referred to as the number system character. The following five digits is a unique item number that you assign to each of your products. The last digit is referred to as a check digit. This number helps scanners determine whether or not the bar code was scanned correctly. The check digit is determined from a mathematical calculation based on the numbers in the manufacturer identification number and item number. Specifically, all of the odd numbered positions of the bar code digits (1, 3, 5, 7, 9, and 11) are added together and multiplied by three. Then all of the even numbered positions of the bar code digits are added together. The totals of both are then added together. The check digit is the number needed to bring that final total to a multiple of 10. (See the figure for more details on how the check digit is calculated.) Each time the UPC bar code is scanned this calculation is performed to ensure the bar code was scanned correctly.

When the bar code is scanned the UPC number is sent to the company's Point of Sale (POS) system to be matched with a price. This way, prices can change as needed without having to alter the UPC bar code.

#26 Obtaining a UPC Code

Jim got himself a UPC Code after his girlfriend told him he was one hot commodity.

UPC Codes are obtained from the Uniform Code Council (UCC). Upon applying for membership at the UCC's web site (http://www.uc-council.org), you would be assigned a company prefix (manufacturer identification number) that makes up part of the bar code number used to identify your products. You can use the prefix, followed by a unique 5-digit number, to create multiple unique bar codes for various products you intend to sell. A new number should be used for each product.

Once you have your unique bar code numbers identified you can have custom labels made for you by a vendor of your choice.

#27 Royalties

Royalties are an effective way of sharing the success of a product while retaining appropriate ownership levels or controlling interest.

Let's use book publishers as an example. You author a book – your concept, your writing. You're just an individual, though, not capable of getting your book to the masses. You submit your manuscript to a publisher, who considers how it fits into their offerings. They accept your manuscript (it usually isn't that easy!), and agree to publish your book.

The relationship with most publishers is that they then take over finishing the book (hiring an illustrator, binding, packaging, pre-selling, selling, and distributing), and take in all payments for sales made. In turn, you (the author) receive royalty payments for your efforts (e.g., 5% of sales), paid quarterly, biannually, or annually.

It's a mutually beneficial relationship. You authored the book. The publisher believes if you enough to spend their resources on publicizing the book and helping to make it successful. They are rewarded for their efforts, as are you. Royalties, in this case, create clear lines of delineation in terms of ownership and marketing rights going forward.

#28 When Your Product Has No Sizzle

The warning signs are typically there when your product isn't performing or selling to your expectations. Lower-than-expected revenue, poor profitability, lack of recognition, and poor reviews are among the factors that tell you that your product has no sizzle.

There are many ways to inject sizzle into your product. Enhance the look of your product. Improve its performance or functionality or usability or adaptability. Begin a new advertising campaign with a fresh look. Have reviews done about the product, which can also act as free advertising.

If you have clients who are already using the product, get to them and encourage them to take a new fresh look at how the product may be improved to be more helpful to them. Your best marketing can come from your current customers, and can be among the many ways to inject the sizzle your product needs.

Financial

Wealth, like happiness, is never attained when sought after directly. It comes as a by-product of providing a useful service.
Henry Ford

#29 Getting Financed
Good business ideas die on the vine because of a lack of financing. Many young companies do not have the financial resources to turn their ideas into profitability. Knowing how to get financed and what type of financial help you want are both extremely important.

The U.S. Small Business Administration (SBA) has terrific loan programs through many SBA lending institutions, with favorable terms and insured loans. "Angel" investors, individuals who invest, are a good way to get financing without having the liability to a bank. Venture Capital (VC) firms typically invest larger amounts but require a larger equity share in what you have built. They also typically require a seat on your Board of Directors.

These three ways of getting financed – traditional loans or SBA loans, angel investment, and venture capital investment – have different strengths and weaknesses, depending on your needs and goals.

#30 Eight Funding Sources
Since finding funding for your business can be quite a challenge! It's helpful to be aware of the various types of financing that are available to entrepreneurs and small businesses. Below is a list of 15 sources of funding for starting and growing your venture.

1. *Bank Loans*
   Commercial loans with fixed interest rates and monthly or quarterly repayment schedules. These can include intermediate-term and long-term loans. Banks typically lend on an asset-based basis or provide operating capital.

2. *SBA Loans*
    The Small Business Administration offers multiple programs which guarantee up to 80% of the loan principal of these term loans provided by banks and commercial lenders.

3. *Equipment Leasing*
    A financing alternative in which equipment is owned by the lender and rented to the business owner at a monthly rate for a specified term. The business owner may purchase the equipment at the end of the lease for fair market value or a predetermined price. The business owner may also choose to continue leasing the equipment or return the equipment and lease new equipment.

4. *Venture Capitalists*
    Institutional or Federal Government funding.

    Institutional venture capital comes from professionally managed funds and is most suitable for companies who can take two million and turn it into ten million in sales in less than five years.

    Federal Government venture capital is provided by Small Business Investment Companies (SBIC) and Specialized Small Business Investment Companies (SSBIC) that provide private capital and additional funds borrowed from SBA-sponsored trusts.

5. *Angel Investors*
    Individuals, rather than companies or institutions, who provide venture capital. More often than not, angel investors help fund early-stage companies.

6. *Initial Public Offering*
    Sale of the company's equity in the form of common stock or shares through an investment banking firm.

7. *Business Incubators*
   House multiple early-stage businesses and offer shared services and reduced rents. Some incubators provide access to low-cost legal, marketing, and other business services.

8. *Royalty Financing*
   Financing through advances against upcoming service and product sales. A portion of the sales is put toward paying back the advance.

#31 Deciding Whether to Apply for Business Credit

In any business, cash is king. Like with your personal finances, it's usually best to only spend what you have and to try and avoid going into debt unnecessarily. There are times, though, when the very best thing you can do for your business is to incur some debt so that you can grow your business.

Also like your personal finances, it's usually best not to jump at the first credit opportunity presented to your business. Take the time to analyze how you plan to pay back whatever debt you incur. If you're using new debt to repay or restructure old debt, thereby expanding your debt, you're simply putting a bandage on a wound that is likely to only get worse. If you can identify revenue that will be generated through expenditures from your new business credit, you have a much better chance of being able to successfully pay down the debt and grow your business.

Use business credit only when you need it. Don't make matters worse by expanding the amount of debt your business is trying to support. If you have a good use for the credit, typically based around revenue growth, that credit can be very helpful.

#32 Debt Financing Options

Early debt financing usually involves securing a bank loan with collateral, such as personal assets, including personal property.

Bank financing can be short- or long-term. Short-term financing can include business credit lines allowing you to borrow up to a maximum amount over a three-year or less period. Long-term financing can be in the form of loans, in many cases secured through the U.S. Small Business Administration (SBA). The term of these loans can be up to seven years, thus reducing your monthly payments but extending the amount of time you will be paying on such a loan.

Many other less common debt-financing options exist. Your commercial lender is many times the best source for determining what options you have.

#33 Equity Financing Options
Equity financing usually means giving up a piece of your company in exchange for financing that will help you to explore more explosive growth options. Equity financing is trading money for stock – plain and simple.

Typically, equity financing comes from three sources – personal investors (angel investors), venture capital firms, or through the sale of stock on the open market (in some cases "going public" through an Initial Public Offering, or IPO), which is usually a later-stage option.

Equity financing can be great because it can involve a great deal of money. It can also be tremendously challenging because you have to give up more to secure equity financing. Research venture capital firms and angel investors on the Internet to learn more about how each organization differs in terms of needs and requirements.

#34 Getting a Loan
You've decided that you need a business loan to grow your business. You have identified ways you are going to turn that debt into profit. You know how you plan to pay your loan back in a timely manner. Now, what do you need to do to get a loan?

Aside from getting loans from friends and family, most young businesses go to a commercial lending institution and request a loan, in many cases secured by the U.S. Small Business Administration (SBA).

These lending institutions have forms for applying for a commercial or SBA loan. They will typically want you to secure the loan amount with collateral, either in the form of personal assets or co-signers with a personal balance sheet to cover your loan amount. If you are willing to put your personal assets, such as property, up to secure your loan, getting a loan will likely be relatively easy. Without securing assets, you may have a difficult time getting a loan. Talk with a commercial loan officer at your bank to learn what they want and need to secure yourself a business loan.

#35 Venture Capital vs. Angel Investment
Venture capital and angel investors typically invest in companies at a larger dollar value than commercial lending institutions. Venture capitalists are organizations with a Board of Directors that help to guide their investment decisions. Angel investors are usually individual investors. Their criteria for investments can vary greatly.

The pros of working with venture capital firms include more available money, a larger organization supporting your efforts, and involvement in your operation, particularly through your Board. Cons include that with greater investment comes greater responsibility and hence greater accountability. Venture capitalists can be impatient and make your life difficult by driving you to work harder in an attempt to help you realize greater success. They can also be so large that you are only a blip on their radar screen and you don't get as much support from them as you anticipated.

The pros of working with angel investors is that you are typically talking about one investor, and that one investor can be a door-opener for your business – someone who helps to generate business in the interest of their own investment. They can be more personal in their approach, and may not dominate your Board. Cons include having smaller financing numbers with which to work, and having the backing of only an individual versus a larger organization.

#36 How Investors Make the Decision to Invest
Not all investors use the same reasoning when deciding to invest in a company – not even close. There are some fairly solid criteria that you need to cover though, to give your company the best chance of being considered for investment.

Investors look at your business plan, and sometimes look at your marketing plan in more detail because they're more concerned about how you're going to make money than on the concept behind the business. In some cases, you'll see investors turn directly to the financial projections in your business plan so that they can gauge the reality of your plan, at least in their eyes.

Investors want to see that you can generate revenue, so you need to prove that there is a market out there for what you're trying to do, and that you know how to get a good enough piece of that market to make their investment worthwhile. Investors are not in it to do you favors, typically – they're in it to make money.

Finally, many investors put the greatest emphasis on the team you have assembled to be part of your operation. They invest in the jockey, not the horse – or they invest in the "A" team with the "B" plan. In other words, if your team has the credentials and history of success, the investor will look much more favorably on your plan.

#37 Financing through Asset Liquidation
Cash-strapped companies that want to improve cash flow might consider selling their business' assets. This can be a

fast way to self-finance although businesses should be cautious about the quick fix and really consider their dependence on assets that might be liquidated.

If you're looking to raise capital but don't want to lose valuable equipment, you can consider a sale/lease-back relationship where you sell your equipment or real estate to another organization for a one-time payment then lease the equipment from that organization. Sale/lease-back relationships create a good source of cash immediately and also offer tax benefits.

Another option for generating immediate cash is financing based on accounts receivable. Essentially, the receivable becomes your asset that can be sold to a third party who collects when the receivables have been received.

The key is to place a value on your assets and analyze your dependency on them. Assets with a high value will obviously be easier to liquidate, but could also pose a greater risk to you if your company has to operate without them. The above options are good ways to keep use of your assets while releasing ownership.

#38 Value Your Privately Held Business
Putting a value on a privately held business is not an exact science. Many factors are involved in a valuation, including in what industry you do business, how much revenue your company generates, the growth curve of your business year-to-year, debt, profitability, products, and your client list, among others.

Different industries can generate inflated valuations. For example, the ".com" era inflated the worth of many businesses, in some cases providing a multiplier of *ten* to the annual revenue of the business. In other words, a company generating one million dollars of annual revenue was valued and sold at ten million dollars. Those are the extreme cases, most of which are now a thing of the past.

The best way to value your privately held business is to work with an independent Certified Valuation Analyst (CVA). They apply as close to a scientific approach as possible, taking into consideration those aforementioned factors and providing you with the most reliable and realistic business valuation.

#39 Hiring an Appraiser/Evaluator
If you're buying a business or having someone invest in your company, a professional appraiser can lend formality and science to what is typically an unscientific transaction. A Certified Valuation Analyst (CVA) is best qualified to establish the relative value of a company. Their work will provide a foundation around which to negotiate final terms.

Appraisals can take place for things other than businesses, of course. Again, professional appraisers are paid to know the industry and relative values within that industry. Where the value of what you have or want fits is determined by a cross-section of criteria, lending science to an arena consisting of estimates.

#40 Stock Options
Stock options are widely used by companies to both reward employees and/or Board members and to secure key staff so that critical turnover is avoided. Stock options are a very good way to involve employees in the business more directly, providing them with convertible ownership in the company.

Stock options typically are provided to staff or Board members as recognition or reward for efforts in helping in the company's success. In most cases, these people are given stock options in the form of convertible shares at a certain price, presumably later convertible at that low price into common stock. Stock options usually have a "shelf life" of three, five, or ten years, and are sometimes given to employees in stages, where more stock options are given the longer the employee stays with the company.

When a company gets bought or goes public, people with stock options can convert their shares at that low price at which they were given, then turn around and sell the shares at a higher purchase or public price, creating a windfall for those holding stock options.

#41 Buying vs. Leasing Equipment
The decision to buy or lease equipment is typically all about cash flow. Purchased equipment can save you finance charges but deplete cash more rapidly. Leasing equipment incorporates monthly payments that include paying interest on that lease.

In many cases, leasing equipment can be done on three-year terms, thus making your monthly payments low, and if interest rates are low, leasing can save your cash. Buying outright eliminates monthly payments but requires full payment, thus affecting cash flow.

Buying vs. leasing comes down to your cash availability, the health of your company, and your corporate goals with regard to leasing.

#42 Accounting Rules of Thumb
There are general accounting rules that apply to almost any type of business. Cash is king in business, and controlling your cash flow is important to the health of your company. As such, one simple rule involves timing the paying of your bills (your payables) versus the timing of being paid by your clients (your receivables.)

Create a payment schedule for your payables so that you're paying them when they're due but not before. Retain your cash for as long as possible. They're not expecting to be paid before your payment due date anyway, so wait and maintain a healthy cash position. Likewise, push your clients (with polite persistence, of course) to pay what they owe you as quickly as possible, again to enhance your cash position. Particularly if your clients are late in payment, it's perfectly acceptable to call them directly and request payment. You provided a product or a service for them. They need to pay their bills.

Another rule involves business leasing. If you're a small business that is cash strapped, leasing can be an excellent option. You'll end up paying more in the long run, but particularly if leasing rates are reasonable, your overall payment won't be that much more, and you'll help your cash position by stringing out payments over a longer period of time. For big-ticket items, rather than have a one-time large outlay, smaller monthly payments can make sense. Be careful, though, that you're not leasing equipment that will only be used for a short time or will become obsolete; you won't like paying over the months for something that you're no longer using.

Finally, for any type of acquisition you may be interested in, whether it's a product or a company or anything else, spend the time and/or money to professionally determine the value of what you're buying. Determine how quickly you can get back out of your acquisition what you put into it.

#43 Choosing the Proper Accounting Method
Almost every business uses one of two methods of accounting: cash or accrual. Work with your accountant to determine which is better for you tax-wise.

Simply put, accounting on a cash basis is just that – what cash you have gained and spent over the course of the year. What cash comes in (or payments hit) over a given month represents your revenue, and what cash goes out (or payments made to pay bills) represents your expenses. On an accrual basis, your revenues are represented by what you bill out, regardless of payments made. If you invoice clients for $50,000 in a month, that part of your income line is $50,000, even if payment doesn't occur until months later. To some, accrual basis more realistically represents the actual flow of business. You do work or sell products, and you invoice your clients. That's when the business hit, and should be reflected accordingly, regardless of when clients pay. That's one way of looking at it. To others, cash is cash and represents the health of a company, again, depending on the type of company.

Businesses that extend credit to their clients, such as allow them net 30-day payment terms, are typically best served using an accrual basis of accounting. On the other hand, businesses that pay and receive payment promptly would benefit most using a cash basis. Cash basis may be easier to understand, but accrual isn't difficult after you start using it. The IRS actually requires companies to use an accrual basis if they maintain large inventories.

Finding and using the talents of a good accountant, particularly a Certified Public Accountant (CPA), can be very beneficial to your business, both in terms of answering your questions and establishing the right methods for your accounting.

#44 Choosing a Calendar or Fiscal Tax Year
Determining whether to operate and account on a calendar or fiscal year is typically dependent on your type of business, the industry in which you compete, or how your largest client(s) operate.

The U.S. Government, for example, does not operate on the calendar year. Thus, if the majority of your business is government business, you may elect to have the same tax year as the Government.

Also, if your business is cyclical, such as working with schools whose business is also clearly cyclical, you may want to account for your business on a non-calendar year basis.

#45 Getting Control of Overhead
Overhead, or indirect expenses, can kill your business. Controlling unnecessary expenses gives you greater opportunity for survival and ultimate success. Every

business must incur overhead expenses, but the very well run businesses know how to control their overhead.

Overhead expenses are basically any expense not related to generating revenue. If you're a service-oriented company, direct labor comes from customers paying for service. If you're product-based, it's about selling products to cover costs associated with the production and sales of your products. Overhead expenses can include executive and administrative support, rent, utilities, and equipment.

Controlling your overhead is controlling expenses. Use only as much administrative support as you need. If managers are not directly billable or directly responsible for production of products, look at how crucial they are to your operation. If you have more space than you need, you may want to look at smaller facilities, which will in turn reduce your utilities. Get control of your overhead expenses and make your company healthier.

#46 Adopt a Conservative Spending Rule

The Jones were so much happier after
they adopted a conservative spending style.

As has been stated elsewhere in this book, in business, cash is king. You don't want to have the burden of carrying and servicing a large debt load. Having good and growing revenue is extremely important in helping to have a healthy company. Equally important is adopting a conservative spending rule and controlling unnecessary expenses.

Some simple rules on adopting conservative spending habits involve asking important questions to help yourself to consider the ramifications of your purchases, including:

- Do we really need it? If it's a "would be nice" purchase, perhaps it's unnecessary.

- Can it wait? If it's something that isn't needed until next quarter, purchase it then, if it's still needed at that time.

- Can we lease it? If it's an expensive item and lease rates are reasonable, it may be better to save the cash outlay and stretch payments over time.

- Are there better deals out there? Comparative shopping can save you money. It always pays to compare.

Even as you begin to realize success and profitability, retain the feeling in your company that you're small, clawing and scratching to save every dime and maximize profits. Usually a simple analysis suffices, particularly if you're in the habit of considering your spending. Don't overdo it and spend too much time saving that dime, because time is money.

#47 All About Shipping

Chances are, if your business sells a product you're going to be faced with shipping to your customer. This can be costly, expensive, and detrimental to your reputation if not done correctly. Keep these five key tips for successful shipping in mind the next time an order goes out:

1. Fast and inexpensive shipping leads to customer satisfaction. Don't sit on the order. Process sales quickly and limit the time spent waiting by the customer.

2. Package your shipment carefully. Quality is important when it comes to delivering your product. You want to make sure goods are not damaged. Use bubble wrap and foam chips as appropriate to protect your customers' orders.

3. Don't depend on one carrier to fulfill all of your shipping orders. There's never a single solution and evaluating your options frequently will save costs.

4. Pay attention to the dimensions of your packages. Exceeding dimensional restrictions can result in increased costs regardless of the weight of your shipment.

5. Don't try to gain profit through overcharging your customers for shipping. Your competitors will win when your prospective clients go elsewhere with their business.

#48 Cost-effective Company Transportation

If you're in a business that requires delivery service or other needs for transportation, you don't necessarily need to run out and lease a vehicle right away. You can cut down your expenses by purchasing a used car and paying for the vehicle with cash. Leasing a vehicle will only result in incurring debt and paying more than you need to.

If you really don't need company transportation that often, consider renting vehicles those few times that you *do* need a car for business. Many businesses located in metropolitan areas will save on the expense of a vehicle and insurance by relying on public transportation to get them to and from places and then rent a vehicle for longer trips.

#49 Six Benefits of Automatic Payroll Deposit

Working with your bank, you can automatically have checks deposited into employees' bank accounts. Benefits include:

1. Eliminates time and resources spent manually processing payroll and distributing checks.

2. Eliminates hassle and expense of replacing lost or stolen checks.

3. Increases employee productivity by eliminating errand runs to the bank to deposit paychecks.

4. Attracts employees – it's a benefit.

5. Peace of mind – checks are deposited automatically and on time.

6. Streamlines audit evidence, making accounting easier.

#50 Five Tips for Beating Check Fraud
If your business accepts payment by check, make sure you follow the tips below to lessen your likelihood of becoming a victim of check fraud.

1. Use check guarantee services consisting of potential negative information on check-writers.

2. Accept debit cards as point of sale.

3. Collect information about your customer. Write down their driver's license information or other identification on the check they provide to you. Consider adding surveillance cameras if you serve walk-in customers.

4. Consider requiring multiple signatures on any outgoing checks that are written.

5. Know what's expected of you. Banks have guidelines for reporting fraud. Make sure you're aware of these guidelines and any other rules that may affect your business.

#51 All About Payroll Taxes

One of the most important things you can do in business is to keep Uncle Sam (a.k.a., the Internal Revenue Service – IRS) happy with timely and accurate payments. It is imperative that you know how and when to pay Social Security and withholding income taxes from employee paychecks.

If you qualify, you can deposit quarterly. If the total withholding is less than $2,500 (as of this printing), the IRS allows businesses to deposit the Social Security and income taxes they withhold from employees every three months. Anything above that $2,500 and the IRS applies other rules (read *IRS Pub. 15 Circular E, Employer's Tax Guide*).

You can also pay electronically with the IRS' Electronic Federal Tax Payment System (EFTPS). Businesses whose annual tax deposits exceed $200,000 are required to use it. Companies can pay these taxes by phone, through the Internet, or with a financial institution. Other companies are encouraged to file and pay electronically to save time and avoid late payment penalties from lost or delayed mail.

The IRS web site (www.irs.gov) contains great detail about everything IRS, including payroll taxes. One of the great features of the site is that it includes employer forms and advice for new and established businesses alike, covering many industries. .

#52 Correcting Tax Mistakes

First, to avoid making tax mistakes, work with a good accountant. If mistakes are made, though, don't worry. Just don't let mistakes linger. When a mistake has been made, fix it, and the IRS or State will be more understanding, knowing that an honest mistake has been made and that an honest effort is being put forth to correct the mistake.

Some simple rules to correcting and/or avoiding tax mistakes include:

- *Use the proper form*
  The IRS web site, www.irs.gov, and most state web sites have the forms you need.

- *Know the deadlines*
  There are different deadlines for submitting tax forms – federal and state forms, monthly, quarterly, and annually.

- *Check rules on amending*
  If amending a return is possible, it is a reasonable and acceptable way of correcting a previous mistake.

- *Stay up to date*
  Check with your accountant or on-line for changes in interest or tax rates.

#53 Exit Strategies

Attention business passengers: Please ignore the man parachuting from the plane. Your possible exit strategies are as follows...

When you have a company, it is important that you have an exit strategy in mind, even from the beginning, and even if you believe you'll be running your company forever. An exit strategy is an important part of any business plan.

Typically, there are three predominant types of exit strategies. You can sell your company, being acquired by someone else. You can attempt to set your company up for an Initial Public Offering (IPO), also called, "going public." You can also be part of a management buyout, where the management team buys parts of the company that they don't already own.

Different strategies work for different situations. If you are experiencing explosive growth, an IPO may create the greatest monetary success. If you have concern over who takes over what you've built, you can control who acquires your company. Exit strategies are defined so that you have goals concerning the successful exit from your company when and if that day comes.

General Business

In the business world, the rearview mirror is always clearer than the windshield.
Warren Buffett

#54 Know Why You're in Business

Ask yourself the necessary question to understand why you're in business. Do you want to work for yourself? Do you have an idea that is unique that you'd like to take to market? Do you want to partner with colleagues who have similar goals and ideals? Why are you doing what you're doing?

If you don't know why you're in business, you may be floundering. You may lack the passion necessary to be leading a business. If you haven't researched your markets sufficiently, you may be headed for disaster. Have an idea, find passion within it, research its potential, and drive hard. Know why you're doing what you're doing.

#55 Traits of a Successful Leader

Successful leaders have similar traits, regardless of industry or type of business. There are differences, of course, but the macro traits of success are strikingly similar.

Most successful leaders are clear in their communications. They make their goals and expectations known and understandable. They stay fit, are generally optimistic, and provide positive feedback to their employees.

Successful leaders work well with other leaders, negotiating for what they want but working toward consensus, creating win-win situations with partners. Leaders lead by example. Actions speak as loudly as words.

#56 Imitate Others Who Are Successful

Role models are important to have, whether you are a kid who looks up to a parent or teacher, a teen who looks up to a musician or athlete, or an adult who looks up to others in or around their industry.

Look at the traits of those you look up to. What makes them successful? What is it about them that you like?

Imitating some of their traits can be a good thing, as long as you remain your own person. Successful people are constantly imitated, usually resulting in good traits being passed on to others.

How they act, what they say, how they say it, how they conduct business – all of these traits and more can help to make you more successful.

#57 Three Myths of Success
Myth #1: You have to play by the rules to be successful.
Reality: Some rules can't be broken. Others can. Differentiation through pushing through limitations is a great way to grow consumers' awareness of your business.

Myth #2: Success is defined by making money.
Reality: You should define how you intend to measure success before you even begin. Success can be measured by the number of jobs you provide the economy, or the number of solutions you provide customers, or the number of years your business has operated. Not every successful entrepreneur is a millionaire.
Myth #3: Success is a goal.
Reality: Success is the result of achieving your goal. It isn't something you strive for or gain without ever accomplishing what you set out to do. Making "being successful" your goal will keep you chasing your tail for years.

#58 The Power of Visualization
Being able to visualize your success is key to becoming successful. This holds true for specifics and long-term goals. From visualizing exactly what you will say to your team to conveying a sense of urgency through completion of a time-sensitive project, the ability to *see* it all and consider your actions before you're faced with a situation is a powerful skill.

Some refer to this ability to visualize as the "helicopter view." You need to set yourself above the project, above the task at hand, above your situation, and look at it from a more global perspective. Being aware of the intricate details is certainly necessary to manage your success, but visualizing the steps between where you are now and where you want to be tomorrow requires hovering above and taking that helicopter perspective.

Visualization also requires you to use your creativity and imagine new and more effective solutions to problems. Don't be afraid to try something that's never been done if you feel it will help you create a successful scenario.

#59 Focusing on Your Potential
One of the most common shared traits of leaders is their ability to assess their own skills and understand their limitations and their potential.

To train yourself to focus on your potential, begin by considering your abilities and acknowledging your inner critic. What types of tasks can you do well? What types of things do you *enjoy* doing, even if you're not particularly good at doing them? Or what types of things *would* you like to do if you knew how? Lastly, consider why you can't do the things you enjoy or would enjoy doing. Your answers will provide a good assessment of your potential.

Now that you have an outline of your potential, use this list and focus on your abilities instead of what you're unable to do. Focusing on your potential instead of your limitations, will help to ensure entrepreneurial success and minimize the number of times you allow your limitations to determine your future.

#60 Building upon Your Strengths
Good leaders are aware of their strengths and focus on building upon them. Surprisingly, few people really pay close attention to their strengths and give more attention to

their limitations. This simply promotes failure rather than encouraging success.

Consider your interests and aptitude for them. These are your strengths. Focusing on things that you have no interest in, or no aptitude for, won't help you to grow. Developing your potential and building upon your strengths requires that you find something you enjoy and that will motivate you to work harder.

You'll know when you're working toward your potentials and building upon your strengths because it won't feel like a chore even if it doesn't happen easily. You'll find yourself improving upon your skills just for the motivation and confidence it brings.

#61 When You Lack Know-how
Since most entrepreneurs are often responsible for wearing many unfamiliar hats, it's no wonder that many small businesses fail as a result of a lack of know-how in a particular aspect of business. Not understanding one factor in business, such as accounting, can be incredibly damaging to the health of your overall company if you're not careful.

So what should you do when you lack know-how? Well for a start, don't be afraid to admit it!

Entrepreneurs who are required to wear several hats and don't understand all aspects of businesses should establish and consult with a board of advisors. The business will benefit from the experience and skills of board members if the right people are involved.

In addition to consulting with directors, you can also create an advisory board that can provide valuable guidance. Advisory board members do not carry the legal or financial liability that directors do, potentially allowing you to recruit advisors more easily.

As an alternative, entrepreneurs can also hire professional consultants hourly or on a retainer and have them be responsible for certain aspects of the business. This, of course, requires a trusting relationship since a lot has been invested in the business. Ask business colleagues if they use any consultants and look for recommendations.

Lastly, you can also solicit the help of business development groups such as the Service Corps of Retired Executives (SCORE). Check with local economic development organizations for other resources that can help you fill knowledge gaps, and eliminate the chance of failure that results from a lack of know-how.

#62 When You Don't Know
A good entrepreneur can admit that he or she doesn't have all of the answers. Those who can't, deny themselves the opportunity to grow through education.

When you don't know what your competitors know...

1. Get involved with industry organizations and associations.

2. Subscribe to industry publications.

3. Attend trade shows and conferences.

4. Purchase top-selling books for your industry.

5. Subscribe to newsgroups and participate in on-line forums related to your industry.

6. Ask your competitors' clients what it is that they like about your competitors.

7. Become a client of your competitor and study their relationship with you.

When you don't know the answer to your clients'
questions...

- Be honest.

- Don't try and fake that you know or have all of the
  answers. You'll be denying yourself an opportunity
  to learn, not to mention you'll be risking your
  credibility and the trust and confidence your client
  has in you.

- If you don't have all of the answers, tell your client
  that you're not sure but that you'll find out. If you
  feel like you would be jeopardizing your client's
  confidence in you by admitting you don't know, tell
  them you have some great information back at the
  office and ask if you can get it to them the next day.
  That will buy you enough time to research the
  question and find an answer to your customer's
  need.

When you don't know where to get the answers...

- When you're faced with an entrepreneurial question
  or problem and you don't know where to get an
  answer or how to solve it, look to community
  resources for small businesses and business
  owners.

- Consult with local universities' business
  departments.

- Consider hiring a business student as an intern for
  free advice and help with your business.

- Consult your community economic development organization for information about local programs and opportunities for community businesses.

- Read entrepreneurial magazines and publications dedicated to informing business owners.

- Look to government resources for assistance such as the Small Business Administration, Internal Revenue Service, your state's insurance department, the Securities and Exchange Commission, and others.

#63 Subscribe to On-line Newsgroups

One of the most informative tools the Internet has been offering for the last ten years are newsgroups. These are essentially electronic bulletin boards where users can post comments or read other users' comments.

If you're looking for industry-specific news, or groups related to specific products, services, or solutions you offer, visit Google.com's directory of newsgroups at http://groups.google.com.

#64 Let Go of Your Fear of Change

In order to grow, you need to let go of your fear of change and be willing to delegate tasks and trust your staff and partners.

Growth isn't something that happens to you or to your business. You have to produce growth. Much like happiness, it's a journey and not a destination. You have to be proactive in your decision to grow by accepting and supporting change.

#65 Successful Mistakes

When you make a mistake, it always helps to think of the situation in a different light and remember that the wrong answer is often the correct answer to a different question. Document your mistakes and the things you learned as a result. That knowledge could be valuable in another situation.

Don't forget that mistakes are simply experiences you never expected to have. Allow yourself permission to fail and experience the unexpected – it's the fuel for growth and change.

The three keys to a successful mistake are:

1. *Making mistakes quickly.*
   If you spend a great deal of time making a decision and you make the wrong one, that's an awful lot of wasted time, wasted money. Don't spend too much time making decisions when the right decision isn't obvious. Allow yourself to pick the wrong decision, but do it quickly.

2. *Recognizing mistakes early.*
   Recognizing mistakes in the early stages will help you save the amount of time and resources you expend on the mistake. If something doesn't seem right, dig deep for the reason and critique your decision. Ask those you trust for "if I were you" opinions. Look at the facts. If the preliminary results of your decision don't support your reasons for making the decision, chances are you're making a mistake.

3. *Remember the mistake.*
   Mistakes are only beneficial in two ways – they encourage growth through experience and teach us what not to do in a similar situation in the future.

#66 Dealing with Business Failures

Recognizing downward trends in business as they're happening can make or break your business. Every business will have failures to some extent – it's how quickly you recognize the situation and how you deal with the failure that will determine how well you will be able to continue.

In many cases, like with the stock market, you may have to determine when the best time is to get out of a situation, thus cutting your losses. Cutting your losses can be as important as benefiting from your successes, as prolonged failure can create corporate pain exponentially.

The reasonably consistent analysis of your company's performance will help you recognize failures before they become substantial.

#67 Deny the Possibility of Failure

The power of positive thinking is an amazing thing. It can take seemingly impossible situations and make them possible. It can affect a team straining to reach its goals and inject the necessary energy to reach a successful end.

Recognize what constitutes failure. By asserting that failure is not an option, you focus on what will make your efforts successful. You won't be wasting your time with negative energy. Instead, you will be driving toward a positive end by not even considering failure to be an option.

#68 Keeping Your Entrepreneurial Spirit Strong in Challenging Times

Every significant effort you undertake will experience challenging times. There are ups and downs with every business effort that means anything, and how you deal with that adversity can influence the success you realize.

In down times, like downturns in the economy, staying true to your entrepreneurial goals and objectives can be difficult. You may want to change how you do business, or exercise your exit strategy. True entrepreneurs with strong spirit hang in there, endure the stormy weather, and stay focused on the macro goals that they are confident will bring them ultimate success.

#69 Beating Procrastination
It's so easy to procrastinate. "I'll do it tomorrow" is a common theme for too many individuals. Limiting or eliminating procrastination can make your company more productive, eliminating wasted time.

One good way to beat procrastination is to have a wide range of tasks for each employee, prioritized from most to least important. People with prioritized tasks are more productive because they're driven to complete the tasks that are in front of them. Burning out on one task is avoided by having others available to work on until the feeling of burnout is gone. This way, everyone stays more focused and productive.

#70 Create an Advisory Board
Companies have Boards of Directors sometimes made up of investors focused on the financial success of the company. While it is critical to track the financial track record and establish financial goals, it is also important to have people you can depend on to provide information and knowledge about your industry.

An advisory board can be made up of experts in your field that focus on the scientific, technological, engineering, or other aspects of your company. They help to ensure that you stay ahead of the game or maintain your unique advantages. Advisory board members don't carry legal or financial liability, making it potentially easier to get them involved.

In small companies, they are typically compensated with non-cash items. In larger companies, cash or stock options are appropriate. A talented Advisory Committee can help you get additional financing as well, showing that you have covered all of your corporate bases in the formation of your company.

#71 Keep the Big Picture in Mind
You might be managing a project, writing a proposal, or having your first meeting with what could be a key client. Don't make things too complicated. Don't sweat the details. Think about what your big goals are and act accordingly.

Some people call it the "helicopter view." If you can hover above your professional universe, you can probably see every aspect of what you do more clearly. Keeping the big picture in mind means driving toward your macro goals and not letting your micro goals slow you down.

#72 Passion = Success
If you aren't passionate about your entrepreneurial efforts and opportunities, you are not going to succeed. It's as simple as that. Particularly if you have stuck your neck out and are trying to make it as an entrepreneur, passion is the only way to win.

Ideally, combining two passions in what you try to do as an entrepreneur will ignite maximum effort and performance. Two passions drive you constantly, and can provide a uniqueness that separates you from the crowd.

#73 Creating a SWOT Analysis
If you aren't familiar with the term, SWOT is an acronym that stands for strengths, weaknesses, opportunities, and threats. Most consultants will perform a SWOT analysis for businesses in preparation for growth. It's a tool used for auditing an organization and its environment and helps you focus on key operating issues.

The results of the SWOT analysis help you to identify your business' niche within your market, your targeted areas of improvement, your competitive advantage, and actions that complement your strengths and opportunities or eliminate weaknesses and threats.

Strengths
Strengths could be something as simple as knowledge, company history and experience, an innovative product or service, or quality processes and procedures.

Weaknesses
Weaknesses could include a lack of marketing expertise, a lack of branding establishment and consumer awareness if you're just getting started, location of your business, or damaged reputation.

Opportunities
Opportunities are external factors and potential areas of growth for your business. For example, creating an on-line presence and selling your products on the web would be considered an opportunity. Becoming a distributor of a like product or service that doesn't compete with your business but shares a target audience could be another opportunity. Other examples include a new international market, a market vacated by an ineffective competitor, mergers, and other strategic alliances.

Threats
Threats are also external factors and could encompass a variety of things. A new competitor in your market, a new and innovative product or service offering from your competitors, or a taxation introduced on your product or service, are all examples of threats.

Once you have identified the strengths, weaknesses, opportunities, and threats of your business, you can base your marketing plan's objectives on your findings. For example, if you discover that one of your weaknesses is the length of time it takes to ship your product, and a threat includes a competitor who ships twice as fast as you, this is an opportunity to gain clientele from improving upon your shipping time. This should become an initiative within your marketing plan.

Key things to remember when conducting a SWOT analysis are:

- Distinguish between where your business is today and where it could be in the future.

- Be realistic about the strengths and weaknesses of your organization.

- Be specific, short, and simple.

- Always use benchmarks for your analysis.

- Remember, it's all subjective.

#74 Constant Benchmarking

One key to quickly growing your business is to establish benchmarks right from the start based on best practices, constantly comparing your progress to your benchmarks. If you measure your performance based on those benchmarks and monitor the results frequently you'll find out if you've gone off track much quicker! Companies who recognize that they've strayed from their goals quickly have a much easier time getting back on track and achieving their goals.

Plan ahead. Document your vision of your business and remain focused. Doing so will give you a competitive advantage and help you realize your goals and eliminate problems before they begin.

#75 Planning for Growth

The key to growing your business is strategic planning, a process, not an end unto itself. Many businesses forgo planning once they have completed the start-up process and have received financing. If you've already developed your business plan and are underway, don't toss planning aside! Adhere to your business plan and your marketing plan and constantly analyze your results with your forecasts. Growth is continuous and requires supervision.

Growing unnecessarily or for the wrong reasons is one of the most common growth traps most entrepreneurs face. Implement "controlled growth" by defining what growth means to you and adapting and reorganizing accordingly. Don't grow for the sake of expansion only, and don't expand for greater prosperity or opportunities you just can't pass up. You can't be everything to everyone so pick your niche based on your competitive advantage and excel at what you do. You don't need to grow your business to provide solutions for your clients – that's what networking and strategic alliances are for!

In summary, to grow successfully you must develop a vision, have a business model in mind, and develop short-term goals to realize your long-term goal. Stick to your plan and don't change it until you've successfully outgrown it!

#76 Process vs. Outcome
When analyzing and growing your business, you should focus on processes and not the outcome. The process is much more important than the outcome because it drives results. As long as you're focused on the outcome, you'll only achieve what you expect to achieve. Focusing on the process opens your business to a world of unlimited possibilities.

#77 Establish Business Goals
Great athletes and sports teams set short- and long-term goals before and even during each season. If you want your business to be great, you need to do the same thing, and because the business landscape sometimes changes rapidly, reassessing your goals during the year can be appropriate.

It is important to have both short- and long-term goals. While long-term goals provide the "big picture" view, short-term goals are the enablers, allowing you to take positive forward steps to reach your long-term goals.

Finally, set realistic goals based on your capabilities, but also reach out and set some significant long-term goals that may seem difficult to achieve but at a place where you would really like to see your company be in future months or years.

#78 Stress Reduction for Entrepreneurs

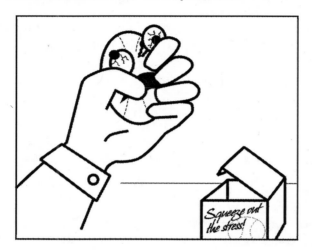

Squeeze out the stress!

Maybe more for entrepreneurs than anyone else, stress can creep into your life. Maybe you've put your personal property up to secure your first business loan. Maybe your whole year depends on successful delivery of a project in two weeks. Maybe you're juggling so many things, your head is spinning. Managing your stress is important, and can be accomplished in both professional and personal ways.

Professionally, monitor your progress by looking at your business goals and how you're doing versus your expectations. Knowledge is key, and knowing how you're doing can help to alleviate stress. Also, don't let important things on your to do list sit idle. Get some things off of your list and it will help you feel productive and reduce stress.

Personally, it is important to do stress-relieving activities, such as exercise or focused relaxation time. Taking time to enjoy yourself or get away can get your professional juices flowing again.

#79 Importance of Key-person Insurance
Every business needs liability insurance to protect against unforeseen events. Not having liability insurance can cripple or devastate your company. Every person should have life insurance to provide for loved ones in case of unfortunate and unexpected death.

Likewise, every business that is serious about doing business should have insurance on its key people. This insurance will protect the company against immediate financial ruin in the case of death of one or more of its key people. Financial protection is enacted to buy the company time to determine the next steps in these cases.

#80 Basic Insurance Needs
Every business needs insurance, both for their employees and for the business itself. Insurance does just what it says – it insures a business against things that could harm its financial stability.

For employees, offering good health care, short-term liability, long-term liability, dental, and life insurance can lure the best employees to your company. For the business itself, business liability can protect the business against unforeseen events. The business can further protect itself against disaster by having key person insurance on those key individuals – thus, should a key person unfortunately pass away, the business would be protected financially so that it could adjust to the change in leadership.

#81 Making Your Company Attractive to Prospective Employees
It is fairly typical that when the economy is good, finding good employees is more difficult than when the economy is

bad. Good economic conditions mean lower unemployment and less availability of good talent. A poor economy produces more good people looking for work.

In past economic booms, for example in the tech sector during the "dot com" era, employers had to create extravagant fringe benefits to attract good people. After the boom was over, employers didn't have to offer more and more because so many good people had been laid-off from other jobs.

During "normal" economic times, employers who offer good health care plans, life insurance, short- and long-term disability, and a 401(k), among other benefits, may have an advantage over companies that offer less. Other important factors in attracting prospects are your location and ability to pay competitive wages.

#82 Hiring Employees – Dos and Don'ts
DO:

- Get to know the personality of the interviewee.

- Learn about his/her background and accomplishments.

- Create an employee handbook and provide a copy to the employee.

- Review state and federal anti-discrimination laws.

- Comply with the Americans with Disabilities Act when hiring.

- Familiarize yourself with employee contracts and determine whether or not they are beneficial to you and your organization.

- Know the legal dos and don'ts of administering pre-employment tests.

- Respect applicants' privacy rights.

- Provide a job description for the employee.

- Make the employee aware of expectations and any benefits.

- Ask if the applicant is legally authorized to work in the country on a full-time basis.

- Provide safe working conditions. Learn more by contacting the Federal Occupational Safety and Health Administration.

- Conduct more than one interview before hiring.

DON'T:

- Discriminate on the basis of race, gender, pregnancy, national origin, religion, disability, marital status, sexual orientation, weight, or age.

- Discuss nationality or ethnicity.

- Discuss age of the interviewee unless you think they may not be legally eligible for employment.

- Ask the interviewee whether or not he/she plans on having children or whether he/she has any already.

- Ask the interviewee about his/her transportation to and from work.

- Ask the interviewee if he/she has ever filed a claim for worker's compensation.

- Discuss the health of the interviewee.

- Discuss the interviewee's current relationship status (i.e. married, divorced, single, etc.).

- Discuss religion or politics.

- Discuss past arrests or convictions.

- Discuss year of graduation or retirement plans.

- Make promises you can't keep when hiring.

#83 Finding Employees

Depending on your industry, you may have different techniques for finding employees. Many employers put advertisements for job openings in their local newspaper, or advertise the opening(s) on-line through a local source. This may create a good volume of candidates for your perusal, though you'd still likely be interviewing and selecting from strangers.

Word of mouth within your company or network is many times the best way to find good employees. These people come with a personal reference from someone within your organization, creating a more immediate confidence that they are of good character and can do the job.

Larger employers sometimes employ "headhunters" – organizations that circulate resumes, matching up skills of individuals in their network with your needs. Headhunters typically get either a set fee or a fee based on a percentage of your future employee's base salary; thus, this method of recruitment can be too costly for smaller companies.

#84 Six POTENTIAL Resume Red Flags

1. Does the resume contain job roles that aren't supported by qualifications?

2. Does the resume list references that can't be followed up with? (i.e. people have moved or businesses have gone under?)

3. Historical length of employment is a good indication of how long you can expect the candidate to work with you. If the employee hasn't stayed very long at other organizations and it appears to be a trend, this may be a red flag.

4. Does the applicant appear to be padding his/her accomplishments?

5. What's missing? Sometimes things are often left out on purpose. For example, if you're looking for a candidate with an extensive educational background and this section is missing from the resume, it may be indicative of a lack of qualifications.

6. Pay attention to accuracy and neatness. If you need an employee who pays attention to detail and he/she hasn't considered errors in his/her resume, chances are this is not the candidate for you.

#85 Topics to Avoid During an Interview
As an employer, it is inappropriate to ask certain things about potential employees. You want to get to know them and what skills they may bring to your team, but you have to be careful where you probe. Asking questions of a more personal nature, regarding their religious or political views or marital status, can not be made pertinent to the job for which they are applying and are thus inappropriate.

As a potential employee, it is likewise in your best interest to avoid certain topics during an interview. Employers may well get turned off to knowing your political or religious views, and you need to be very careful in the presentation of humor.

In both cases as an employer and employee, stick with topics specific to and surrounding the job being considered. Don't stray into areas of potential controversy. It could well create more harm than good.

#86 Employer Identification Number
An Employer Identification Number is issued by the Federal Government and used to identify your business.

When do you need an EIN? You should apply for an EIN if:

You have an employee.

You operate your business as a corporation or partnership.

You file any of these tax returns: Employment, Excise, or Alcohol, Tobacco and Firearms.

You withhold taxes on income, other than wages, paid to a non-resident alien.

You have a Keogh plan.

You're involved with any of the following types of organizations:
Trusts, except certain grantor-owned revocable trusts, IRAs, Exempt Organization Business Income Tax Returns.

Estates.

Real estate mortgage investment conduits.

Non-profit organizations.

Farmers' cooperatives.

Plan administrators.

If none of the statements above describe you or your business, or you're a sole proprietor and have no employees, you're not required to obtain an Employer Identification Number. However, an EIN *does* look more professional on invoices than using your Social Security Number.

#87 Obtaining an Employer Identification Number
To apply for an Employer Identification Number (EIN), the IRS requires you to fill out form SS-4 that can be obtained from their web site at www.irs.gov.

You can obtain an EIN quickly by applying on-line or by calling the Tele-TIN phone number specific to your state. You can also fax your completed application to your service center and expect a return fax within a week. Be sure to include your return fax number!

If you apply via postal mail, be sure to send your completed SS-4 form four to five weeks prior to when you'll need your EIN.

For service center contact information, visit www.irs.gov.

#88 The Contractor vs. Full-Time Employee
You're a business owner trying to build a business while minimizing unnecessary expenses, maximizing revenue potential, and realizing terrific profits. For many companies, particularly service companies, the single largest expense line item on your profit and loss statement is payroll, or a combination of payroll and outside services or consultants.

When should you bring on a consultant? When does it make sense to bring on another employee? The quick answer to both these questions is that when you only need short-term help, use a consultant, and if you have six months or more of foreseeable, supportable work, it's reasonably safe to bring on an employee.

There is, of course, middle ground, where you think you will probably have sustainable work and would like to bring on someone as an employee, but there is risk involved. In this case, you could start them as a consultant, making clear that your hope and expectation is that the work will evolve into full-time employment status, but that there is a chance that won't happen. That way, your position is clear, and they have the situation in mind so that there are no surprises.

The benefits of adding someone as a full-time employee include their dedication, having long-range vision, and being a part of the corporate family. The benefits of adding a consultant include having their specific expertise for the tasks at hand, not having to retain them after the project is completed, and saving on payroll taxes and benefits. Consultants are typically not as loyal to your corporate goals as employees, and many times have tasks beyond your work, as they work with several clients for survival purposes.

Adding a consultant or full-time employee is dependent on the situation at hand. Analyze the short- or long-term implications of adding each and your answer should be clear.

#89 Using Contracts When Working with Consultants
In many cases, consultants you may use are also friends or colleagues in your network. When going to these consultants with opportunities, you may describe the opportunity and plan to work together on a particular job. The deal between you and the consultant may have to happen quickly because of time constraints set by your client.

As a result, you may think that a formal contract between you and your consultant is not necessary, be it because you know them well, the timeline is tight, or the job is relatively small. Regardless, create a standard contract for working with consultants and use it.

No matter how well you like your consultants, the relationship can turn ugly quickly if deadlines are missed or budgets are exceeded. Protect your company legally and financially by adding formality to the relationship with a consultant no matter how well you know or like them.

#90 Employee Contracts
Employee contracts are most commonly used to define and secure the relationship between employee and employer. Employees want stability – to know that they're wanted and needed and that the employer is committed to having them be a part of the organization for a period of time. Employers also want stability – to know that their key staff will remain committed to the effort over the same period of time. Employee contracts can formalize and make legal such desires.

Caution must be used in employee contracts, though. Both parties must make sure they're truly willing to commit to a relationship over an established period of time. Most employees do not have employee contracts. Most employers do not offer their employees contracts. Employees are established as "at will" employees, able to leave their job freely. Likewise, employers are able to release at will employees from their duties freely. An employment contract puts guidelines around the relationship, restricting the freedom of at will employment in a legally binding document.

However, for those employee-employer relationships where both parties want to define and solidify a situation that they mutually feel will continue to be beneficial into the future, an employment contract can make good sense. It can provide a peace of mind and stability to a relationship where both parties are focused on the business tasks at hand rather than employment status.

#91 Non-disclosure Agreements

Non-disclosure agreements are a commonly used legal document between organizations and/or individuals that help to keep sensitive or confidential information or materials private – between only those entering the agreement.

A non-disclosure agreement can protect you in cases where you have an idea, product, concept, plan, or project that is unique and don't want others to share the details of it. It can also be used by your client, for example, where they impose restrictions on your use of their branding, materials, or even their name.

Have your attorney create a standard non-disclosure agreement, one that can be customized for different uses. If another party requires that you use their agreement, like with any agreement, have your attorney review it to ensure that you are protected in every way.

Even if you want to divulge your confidential information to a friend in another company, it's important to lend formality to that relationship through a non-disclosure agreement. Protect what's legally yours in all cases.

#92 Working with Vendors

Vendors provide you and your company with services or products. They become your partners in many ways because you need what vendors provide and in some cases, they provide to you on a regular basis. That regularity creates a comfort zone for both you and your vendor.

That comfort zone can be a plus because it's more enjoyable doing business with people with which you enjoy working. The regularity of your contact with them may allow them to "cut you a deal" every now and then, further solidifying your relationship.

Don't be afraid, however, to take your vendors to task to ensure that you are continuously getting the best value for the best price. Friendships are nice, but they don't pay the bills, and your number one concern must be the financial health of your company, and its ability to provide the very best quality products or services.

#93 The Pros and Cons of Hiring an Intern

Ironically enough, while this book was being written we were in the process of bringing on an intern to assist with marketing an event we were hosting. This student was looking for some experience over her holiday break and it seemed like a very good match for us both. Unfortunately, after investing in computer hardware and taking time to set everything up for her to be able to jump in with both feet, she decided to stay with her family for the holiday.

Although internships can often bring great people into your business and add value and high-quality work to the table, that's not always the case. Sometimes interns are a challenge to keep motivated or they simply aren't ready for the opportunity.

While interns bring numerous benefits to your company from offloading full-time employees to potentially becoming full-time employees themselves, it's important that you keep your expectations limited and flexible, and always strive to understand what motivates your intern.

#94 Five Steps to Hiring an Intern

Identify your goals in hiring an intern and the needs an intern can fill without jeopardizing your business if things do not go as well as you hope.

Write a job description for each position or role that you identify as an opportunity for an internship position and provide it to local media, colleges, universities, and other organizations. Include a description of skills and duties required to perform the job. This will help guide the intern as well as help you to focus on the intern's responsibilities.

Create an application and make it available for all internship opportunities. Don't forget to include a consent form for applicants to sign to grant you permission to do a background check on them if you so desire.

Interview all applicants before making a selection. This will help you to determine what motivates the individual since they won't be receiving monetary reward for their work.

Hire an intern that you know you can train and keep motivated but keep your expectations realistic.

#95 What to Look for in an Administrative Assistant

A good administrative assistant can be absolutely critical to the success of your organization. If they answer the phone when calls come in, they are the first impression that callers, in many cases clients, get about your company. When the Administrative Assistant answers, their demeanor sets the tone, and their knowledge on how to direct the call or find answers is critical. People don't like getting bounced around, and a good Administrative Assistant knows what's going on and where, to direct traffic effectively.

In larger companies, an Administrative Assistant may be a central point for many employees. Their ability to juggle questions, or people just coming up to chat, or requests for things like copies or binding or other administrative tasks, can make or break the efficiency of a company.

Your company may be large enough where you don't need an Administrative Assistant to do more than answer phones and make copies. In those cases, what to look for is friendliness and efficiency. If you expect to need them to do more, you may want to review specific skills, such as knowledge of word processing or spreadsheet tools, the Internet, and more.

#96 Hiring Janitorial Services

Considering janitorial staff is usually in your place of business after hours and unsupervised. It's important that you select an individual or company that is reputable, trustworthy, and reliable. Ask your colleagues or others you know and respect who they have hired. Solicit recommendations and follow up with references.

It's also important that you have a clear idea of what type of cleaning assistance you would like prior to interviewing and hiring. Create a list of the types of assistance you need and ensure that the company or individual you hire is willing and able to perform this service.

Lastly, although most basic insurance plans cover outside help, be sure that you have a plan that provides adequate coverage for external help, such as janitorial services, in the event that there is an accident or injury. Better safe than sorry!

#97 Employee Manuals

Employee manuals are particularly important when you start getting more than a couple of employees. These manuals define your company and its policies, policies such as vacation time, unpaid leave, and computer use.

Employee manuals may not constitute a contract between employer and employee. Check with your attorney for state-specific regulations. In most cases, employees are "at will." They are subject to employment status change at the whim of the employer, and are told of that fact along with other corporate policies within an employee manual.

Having each employee sign off on having read and reviewed the employee manual is a good idea, as it constitutes their knowledge of the policies and procedures detailed therein.

#98 Motivating Your Employees
Unmotivated employees will spell the downfall and eventual death of your company. Keeping employees motivated over long periods of time can clearly be challenging. Work goes through a typical ebb and flow, and as an employer and manager of people, you must stay ahead of the game, being proactive in providing motivation at appropriate times.

Motivating can be tricky. You don't want to do it so much that it becomes irrelevant. And you don't want to wait so long to do it that burnout occurs and the motivation is rendered useless. It's also important to motivate to the appropriate level. In other words, don't insult the employee's intelligence with the type of motivation. Don't be condescending, or too much of a cheerleader where it's too sugary-sweet.

Motivation can be found in many different forms – days off, bonuses, new equipment, and recognition, among others. Motivation can be much more simple than that, though. Noting a good job, expressing concern, and being willing to help can get unmotivated people back on track, simply by showing that you care.

#99 The Art of Delegation
You can't do everything. If you're already busy, building your business, growing, and being successful, you simply can't do everything. You also can't expect everyone to do things exactly as you would do it. The challenge in learning how to delegate involves determining *when* to delegate, *what* to delegate, and *to whom* to delegate.

When does it make sense to delegate? The answer is

simple – when you can't do it all yourself.

What do you delegate? Pick tasks that you're willing to give up – perhaps less critical tasks that don't need your personal touch. By focusing on the important and not the urgent, you can maintain focus on those tasks where you can have the greatest impact. Otherwise, delegate.

To whom do you delegate? Understanding the strengths of others is key in determining the answer to this question. Match the task you're trying to delegate with the strength of the person to whom you're delegating, and the task has a higher probability of being addressed, as you would like.

Finally, when you have identified when, what, and to whom you will delegate, make expectations very clear regarding the task at hand. Whoever you're delegating to will handle the task more effectively if they know precisely what's expected and what represents success.

#100 Five Causes of Employee Conflict
Cohesive teams are the most productive, and when in sync, create a good atmosphere in which to work. It is impossible, though, to avoid conflict between employees. Five causes of employee conflict are:

1. Competition – for a job or task, or rise up the corporate ladder.

2. Jealousy – about what each other is getting or doing.

3. Territory – infringement on others' domains.

4. Miscommunication – for example, using e-mail when face-to-face is needed.

5. Losing focus on macro corporate goals – being unnecessarily petty.

Keeping the big picture in mind and communicating openly and immediately, not letting friction build, will help to avoid these and other potential conflicts between employees.

#101 Creating a Safe Workplace
Failure to create a safe workplace for your employees could destroy your business. Accidents cost money and time that most businesses can't afford.

All employers, regardless of the number of employees, must follow federal Occupational Safety and Health Administration (OSHA) standards. Some state standards may be enforced as well.

Beyond general standards that apply to all, the standards to which you must adhere depend upon the industry in which you work. It's important that you learn which regulations apply to you. General standards have specific requirements regarding exits, ventilation systems, hazardous materials, first aid, and fire safety among others.

Under OSHA, it is your responsibility to maintain a safe workplace. Your insurance company may be able to make specific recommendations to help improve upon the safety of your environment. You can also look for related safety seminars in your community. Get educated and save yourself potential loss from workplace accidents!

#102 Giving Employees a Stake in the Business
Employers need to devise ways to energize their staff and keep key employees on board. Giving employees a "piece of the pie" is a way to energize, engage, and commit staff to the company's future.

Typically, employers will provide this incentive through stock options, in many cases vested over a period of time, such as 3-5 years. This energizes employees with the potential for ownership while committing them to the future success of the company by having additional stock options vest over time.

Be careful, though, to reward those that you feel will be an important part of your business for years to come. Take your time in deciding when and how to implement this incentive.

#103 Conducting Performance Reviews

Performance reviews are something that should be done on at least an annual basis. How you conduct performance reviews can help to establish your company as professional, as it reflects directly on your thoroughness as a manager and how you manage and/or communicate with your people.

Performance reviews should never be a surprise to your employees, because communication should be consistent through the year. In many cases, it is a good idea to have the employee write their own performance reviews so that you can compare viewpoints between employee and manager.

Conducting performance reviews should be the presentation of a straightforward list of accomplishments from the prior year, strengths and weaknesses, and objectives for the next year. The performance review is an opportunity like no other for the manager to let the employee know exactly how they are doing.

#104 Knowing When to Fire Your Employees

You usually know when it's time to fire an employee. Poor performance over time or a drastic and negative change in their performance will make you think that it's time to fire them. It's not an easy thing to do, though, because it's a very personal thing. It's also important to outline to the employee the reason(s) for firing him or her so that there are no surprises. You need to be clear as to why the firing is occurring, including details regarding poor performance over time.

When you know it's time and have your documentation lined up to support the employee's release, do so immediately, factually, and unemotionally. If you have provided them with written warnings, not only will you know that it's time, they will, too. It's important not to let bad situations exist for very long within your company. Take care of things promptly, including firing employees, when necessary.

#105 Protecting Yourself When Terminating Employees

Using the "three strikes" rule is always a safe and effective way of firing an employee, and it helps to indicate that it is truly time to do so. Each "strike" consists of a written warning explaining how the employee is underachieving as well as precisely what actions you expect them to take to improve. If there has been little to no improvement in areas of need, after three strikes, you have clear documentation to use in the employee's release. There will be no surprises and they will likely see it coming, creating a less abrasive and uncomfortable situation.

Most companies do not offer employment contracts. They may have an employee manual, but have only "at will" employees, giving both the employer and employee flexibility in hiring, firing, and resigning. As such, as an employer, firing an employee, so long as they know that they are "at will," will provide all of the protection you need when terminating an employee.

#106 Expanding Your Business Space

Growth is a wonderful thing in the world of business! If you're outgrowing your business space and considering adding additional facilities or relocating, chances are you're doing something right and you're doing it well. It's important, though, that you grow cautiously and don't overextend.

When considering expanding to a new location or adding

additional locations, ask yourself whether or not the additional space will generate more revenue for your business. Growing to serve externally verses growing to accommodate internally is the key to expansion.

When considering business space, remember that location and your prospective customers are everything. If your business caters to youth, look for additional space on campus grounds or other high traffic areas frequented by your target audience. Consider ease of access and parking options, too.

Let your prospective customers' needs, behaviors, and motivations have key influence in determining where you set up shop. After all, their business drives your success.

#107 Office Appearance
Particularly if you have an office where visitors occasionally or frequently visit, office appearance is very important because it reflects directly on your company. Having a professional looking office creates a professional atmosphere for visitors and staff alike.

For first-time visitors, first impressions are extremely important. A neat and professional office declares that you are an organized and professional organization capable of supporting others' endeavors in a similar manner. A sloppy office, even in a shipping area, can reflect negatively and give others the impression that you operate in more of a haphazard way.

Keep your office up-to-date. Show off your more recent work, and provide a more modern appearance. Style is important to some that will visit, so it should be to you.

#108 Redundancy
Your important documents, whether they're on paper or electronic, need to be stored in multiple locations to protect against unexpected loss caused by disasters such as fire or power fluctuations/outages. Almost everything in your

office should be protected. Prime candidates for redundancy include:

- Corporate paper-based files, such as employee files, by-laws, Board meeting minutes, etc.

- Tax documents, including all annual returns.

- Corporate accounting files.

- Client files, both electronic and paper-based.

- Important project work.

- Copies of key inventory items and records with originals retained in a safe deposit box or other secure storage facility.

Establishing this level of redundancy is best accomplished by having an off-site location to store your materials. Don't allow one disaster to cause you to permanently lose information critical to your company's past, current, or future success.

#108 Redundancy
Did we mention the importance of redundancy when it comes to storing important company documents?

#109 Storing Confidential Information
The leaking of confidential information can be detrimental if not fatal to your business. Secure storing of your confidential information, both on-line and in print materials, is critical. Drawbacks to confidential leaks could include:

- *Salary information*
  No employee has ever been better off knowing someone else's salary. This information should be kept in secure employee files.

- *Pricing data*
  Either in the form of proposals or quotes, a price list or bid that lands in the wrong hands can hurt or eliminate a potential competitive advantage.

- *Contracts*
  Any contract, whether with a client or contractor or supplier, contains specific information about how you do business with others. Again, in the wrong hands, this information can harm competitive advantages you may have.

- *Project or project information*
  Either in electronic or print format, some projects or product, particularly those with which you have confidentiality agreements, must be kept confidential. If they are leaked, the potential is there for not only you to be harmed but your clients as well.

Storing confidential information is straightforward but not everybody does it and should. For print materials, store your confidential information in a secure, locked, and fireproof cabinet. Only a few, trusted people should have access to the cabinets. For electronic materials, you must first start with a secure server to keep hackers from breaking in from the outside. Firewalls are the most common way of keeping electronic strangers out. Your next step is to keep employees from seeing information you aim to keep internally confidential. Having an Intranet with a domain server is one way to go, allowing you to set specific accesses to specific folders by login name and password.

#110 Purchasing Options for Office Supplies
If you've already purchased supplies for your office then you already know that they can add up – especially if you're going through them quickly and need to restock often.

There are several purchasing options that can help you to save money:

First, consider buying frequently bought items in wholesale or bulk. You can find wholesale distributors on the Internet or at any of the large buying clubs or membership warehouses like SAM'S CLUB or Costco Wholesale Corporation.

Second, you can often find used equipment or an overstock of supplies being sold in local classifieds or auctioned on web sites such as www.ebay.com. Just don't forget to consider the costs of shipping when estimating total costs!

Lastly, always price shop. If you're purchasing large quantities or expensive equipment, compare product reviews and pricing. There are numerous web sites including www.mysimon.com and www.consumerreports.org that have reviews of products that can help you in making the best purchasing decisions. You can also compare prices and make sure you're getting a good buy with sites such as www.pricegrabber.com or www.pricescan.com. Compare and be aware!

#111 Conflict Management
When conflict happens in a business environment, the most important thing you as a manager can do is to address the conflict directly as soon as possible. Conflict that exists for longer periods of time can grow into unmanageable problems.

Addressing the conflict immediately and factually, serving as a moderator able to hear both sides, will help to expedite a solution. Take the personal aspect of any conflict out of it, while addressing the facts as they related to the success of the company instead.

You may have to make a tough decision by agreeing with one person or group and disagreeing with the other. When doing so, make your decision based on facts and corporate goals, and the conflict will be solved or possibly averted.

#112 Curtailing Conversation

Being able to politely end a conversation that has gone on too long is an art, and it will save you distress when you can control your schedule better by doing so. You'll no doubt get into conversations where someone is trying to tell you how the watch was made when all you asked for was the time, and knowing how to get out of it makes you more efficient. Doing so with style helps you avoid insulting someone.

Rather than abruptly end a conversation in frustration, kill them with kindness while still achieving your goal. "I appreciate the information, but I really must go," is perfectly polite, gets your point across, and ends the conversation. It can be that simple. If you're at a conference, you don't want one person to take up all of your time when others may want some of your time. "I'd like to continue this conversation later," is a good way of transitioning out of a conversation while being able to get to others waiting for you.

#113 Choosing a Compatible Business Partner

Partnerships can be extremely beneficial, but you have to be careful, because they can also be a tremendous headache. The best way to think of it is that a business partnership can be very much like a marriage.

A good business partner can make a small business larger, more capable, and more able to acquire more business. A bad business partner can make everything difficult, from completing a job on time to representing you in a less-than-desirable manner.

A successful business partner is typically an individual and/or company that you get along with as well as someone with discernable and complimentary skills to those of you and your company.

#114 Buying a Business
You can strengthen your business greatly through acquisition. Buying another business can rapidly grow your business or address a need. Purchase price is important, as is what you're getting in terms of personnel, products, and style.

Price has to fit what you can afford. Don't be anxious to buy. Negotiation skills are important, just like buying a car. The more patient you are, and if you are able to walk away from the deal, the more likely you are to get the deal you want.

Incorporating another business' personnel can be tricky if the personality of your company is in conflict with that of the company you're acquiring. Spend time to bring people together, as effective team building can make the interpersonal part of the acquisition work.

Your business presumably recognized that this particular acquisition would complement your corporate goals and objectives. Make those goals and objectives clear to everyone, so that there is a true team effort in helping the new business to become part of your business successfully.

#115 Risks of Mergers
Unlike an acquisition where one company buys another and assumes control, a merger is a coming together of companies with splitting up of responsibility and management between the merged companies. Mergers are like a marriage, so you'd better make sure you want this marriage before you commit.

Risks of mergers include:

- Differences in personnel management.

- Differences in marketing strategy.

- Differences in how human resources are handled.

- The feeling that one "good" company has merged with one "bad" company and one is carrying the other.

- Commitment to management in one company but not the other.

Communicating with employees before the merger is finalized creates buy-in. Soliciting opinion and comment helps employees to feel a part of the process. Management must take the time necessary to consider all of the marriage-like elements of the merger to ensure that it can be done for the best interests of all involved.

#116 Dependability – The Key to Service-oriented Businesses

If you're a service business, the most important elements to your business involve your customer focus. You will not succeed as a service-oriented business without complete and utter focus on the customer. Being dependable, honest, hard working, and delivering quality service at a good value are extremely important to your success and your customers'.

In the ideal situation, you as a service business become virtual partners with your customers, almost a part of their organization. They come to depend on you as regular contributors to their success. In turn, your dependability creates that commitment. If they can't depend on you, they won't, and they'll find someone else that they can depend on. Together with the other factors listed, by being dependable, you become one of them – the ideal situation for a service-oriented business.

#117 Delivering Service Late
It's difficult to deliver everything on time. There are times when, for reasons beyond your control, something is going to be late. When that happens, dealing with it is important to how your client feels about you and how likely you are to get more business from them.

As soon as you recognize that you're going to deliver late, let the client know right away, as honestly as possible. Being up front that despite your efforts, things are going to be late will typically go a long way with the client. If you have been a good communicator with the client throughout your relationship, they will be more understanding because of your continued honesty, knowing that being late was because of factors not considered when the initial deadline was set.

#118 Viewing the Client from the Long-term Picture
Don't be exclusively reactive to the needs of your clients. Of course, there are situations where you need to react to them. When you can have the big picture of your client in mind – when you can put yourself in their shoes – you will be able to support them more effectively.

Likewise, viewing your clients with *your* long-term picture in mind allows you to continue to focus on your corporate goals while addressing their long-term goals. In some ways, your company gets in sync with theirs. They drive a part of your business, after all. It only makes sense, keeping your long-term goals in mind, that you view your client from the long-term picture.

#119 When to Let Your Customers Go
You can't keep all of your customers forever. For whatever reason, whether it's disagreements, mergers, acquisitions, relocations, losing to a competitor, or the passing of time, customers are going to leave you. There are times when

you are going to have to let a customer go. Some times and reasons to consider letting customers go include:

- If your customer is demanding too much of your time, as it relates to how much you are compensated for your efforts. In other words, if you are no longer making money working with them, you may want to end your relationship.

- If your business focus or theirs has changed so that you are no longer in sync, don't force a continuation of the relationship – end it.

- If you are no longer able to support your customer the way you have in the past, realize your shortcoming, be up-front with your customer, and suggest that they find someone more able to support their needs.

- If your customer has been acquired and your new primary contact is someone you do not get along well with, don't force yourself to work with someone you don't like – end the relationship, if you can afford, as a business, to do so.

#120 The Importance of Not Burning Bridges

In this case, burning bridges refers to ending a relationship permanently. You may have a customer or a potential customer that is simply a pain, and a persistent pain at that. You're nearing the end of a project and you have a decision to make. Do you tell them how you feel? Will clearing the air help? Will getting things off your chest help you or them?

Over the course of your professional life, you'll almost certainly burn a bridge or two. You can't please all of the people all of the time. However, it can't be overstated that it is important to try not to burn bridges with people, almost in all possible cases.

Simply put, you never know. You never know for sure how the business landscape will change and you may want a relationship with them again. You never know how they or their feelings may change. Exit situations gracefully, without burning bridges. You may never talk with that person or company again, but if you do, you want the doors to be opened, not closed. It makes sense in very rare cases to burn bridges and permanently bury a relationship.

#121 Finding New Customers

If it were easy to find new customers, every business would be thriving. For most businesses, finding new customers is key to their ongoing success. Having one or two good customers that can provide much of your work or revenue is a great thing, but they eventually go away and you need new customers to fill that void.

The trick is how do you find those new customers? Some possible ways include:

- *Stay within the industry.*
  If you've done well in one industry with one or two customers, try to replicate your success with other clients in the same industry. You'll have direct experience in that industry, helping to customize your initial contact, bid, relationships, and work.

- *Play to your strengths.*
  Analyze your company's strengths and other markets in which you may be able to create success. Design a plan to show off those strengths in marketing efforts within those other markets.

- *Ask your employees.*
  Nobody knows your business better than your employees do. Perhaps they've never been asked to think about finding new customers, but many times they have terrific ideas because they know what you're capable of doing.

- *Use your network.*
  Outside of your employees, nobody knows your business better than those in your close outside-of-the-company network do. Those others in your network usually have access to clients you don't, and may be able to help either get you in with other companies or identify possibilities you may not have considered.

- *Use traditional marketing efforts.*
  To reach new people, you have to make contact one way or another. Traditional marketing efforts, including direct mailing, phoning, using the Internet, and attending trade shows, can help make that initial contact and begin a relationship. The relationship may take months or years to develop, but you need people in the queue to develop over time into customers.

#122 Business Travel

Many business travelers are finicky. They want things to be a certain way, from parking at the airport to the seat they're in on the plane to their type of rental car and hotel. Thanks to the many enhancements in making travel arrangements, such as on-line reservations and booking, travelers can be as finicky as they want.

What are your preferences? Do you want the cheapest flight, or do you want to fly First Class? Do you need a compact, midsize, luxury, or other automobile rental? Does your hotel need a fitness room, business center, and/or room service?

Both you and a travel agent have access to the ability to be very specific in your wants and needs. If you do it yourself, shop and compare at the many on-line options, from all-in-one travel centers to the airlines, rental car agencies, and hotels directly. Book your flight 14 days in advance and save on airfare.

Increased security at airports requires more of your time to get checked in. Be sure to leave enough time to do so comfortably. During times of bad weather, call ahead to make sure your flight is departing on time.

During business travel, it pays to begin with the mindset of being patient. You may start your day with traffic to get to the airport, have to park in long-term parking, wait for a shuttle bus to take you to the airport, wait in line to check in, walk to your gate, wait for your flight, wait to board the plane, fly, wait to get off the plane, wait in line to pick up a rental car, deal with more traffic, wait to check in at a hotel, and wait for room service. You get the idea. Patience, in travel, is truly a virtue. Joining particular travel clubs that reward frequent travel can reduce some of that wait and/or personalize your experience.

#123 Car Rental
Business typically looks at car rental in one of two ways – best price or most convenience. Your preference may have to do with where you typically rent – at major airports or at a location within the downtown area of a big city.

Economy car rental companies can save you money but are not always convenient because they don't have the prime locations at major airports or don't have the best customer service. Larger rental companies may have higher prices but may save you time and money through the convenience of their pick-up and drop-off services.

Clubs that can be joined through car rental companies can also save you time and sometimes money by being a frequent renter. If you travel frequently, joining a rental car club could be a good way to reap benefits.

#124 Hotels

Hotels are all about service, and your personal preferences should be most taken into consideration when choosing a hotel. If you care most about price, that narrows down the possibilities. If it's about convenience and location, that further narrows your search. Many hotels offer some kind of rewards program for frequent stays, convertible into prizes, credits, or gifts later.

The sophistication of web-based searches through on-line travel agencies or hotel chains allows you to be as selective as you care to be. If you want to stay near a hotel that has high-speed Internet access and a fitness room, you can select those criteria to narrow your search. If you want a hotel that offers room service or if you're just wanting to sleep there, you can make those choices either on-line or by calling particular hotels.

If you're a creature of habit and have a regular travel schedule, establishing the hotel can result in discounts and rewards for you, all while allowing you to stay where you wanted to stay in the first place.

#125 The Art of Negotiation

Art is the operative word when it comes to negotiation. Good negotiators, simply put, get what they want. In many cases, they make agreements that appear to be mutually beneficial, but in the end, good negotiators make agreements that get them what they want.

Some are "nice guy" negotiators, while some are "bad guy" negotiators. There are times when two people tag-team with one playing nice guy and one playing bad guy. In the end, you should be comfortable with how you negotiate, striving to get what you want.

The keys to effective negotiation are:

- *Information*
  In a negotiation, information is ammunition,
  providing you with the opportunity to answer
  questions and concerns, or position your case to
  your favor.

- *Communication*
  How you present yourself and your position is an
  extremely persuasive way of getting what you want.

- *Patience*
  The more patient you are, in almost all cases, the
  closer a deal will come to what you want.

When you're buying a new car, first you research about the
car – the model, the list price, the dealer cost, the features,
etc. That's your ammo. You're prepared. You go into the
dealership and communicate what you want. The
salesperson tells you what they can sell the car for –
typically the list price. You make clear that you know the
dealer cost and are prepared to pay some percentage over
cost, explaining that you realize that they need to make
some money, too.

This is where patience kicks in. Everybody's experienced
it. "I need to talk to my manager," says the salesperson.
You wait. Several minutes later, the salesperson comes
back and says that they can't do it for what you want, but
that they can go part of the way. Be patient. Stick to your
guns, explaining that you're not trying to be rude, but that
you're perfectly prepared to go to another dealer. "I need
to talk to my manager again," a slightly exasperated
salesperson says. Minutes later, they may even come back
with the manager. A smart dealership will know that you've
done your homework and you will walk soon so they will
give you what you want. A not-so-smart dealership will
continue this negotiation, also known as a hassle at this
point. One way or another, you're done. Either you're

walking or you're buying at the price you want. You've won, because you established your guidelines and stuck with them throughout the negotiation, not being a jerk about it, but being firm.

This applies to virtually any negotiation. Be polite, but stick to your guns, be patient, and be prepared to combat with information. You'll get what you want.

#126 Presentations
In very few instances will you have an opportunity to impress upon many something of importance. An effective presentation can give a group of people the right kind of impression – that you know what you're talking about and that they should do business with you as a result.

Putting together and giving a good presentation is easy, and includes the following steps:

- Know your subject matter.

- Know how much time you have.

- Know your audience.

- Rehearse what you want to say.

- If you're using an aid, such as Microsoft® PowerPoint®, make sure it helps to guide the presentation but doesn't dominate it. People want to hear from you, not read the screen.

- Allow time for questions and answers.

- Provide contact information.

- Be prompt.

#127 The Power of Bartering

If your business is cash-strapped but you have other free resources (time, idle staff, etc.) consider growing your business through bartering. You can put those free resources too good use through offering them in exchange for other business assets or services and products.

We've bartered services for a variety of resources including accommodations, advertisement placement, software, signage, print work, and even computer network installation services! If you think creatively, you can gain a number of resources for time and energy rather than money.

If you would like to learn more about bartering opportunities that are available, there are a few sites on the web which provide a matching service between companies:

- www.barteringconnection.com
- www.ibart.com
- www.barteriton-line.com

You can also search for "trade" or "barter resources" for business on any of the major search engines for more resources.

If you're new to the concept, start with your business alliances, colleagues, and members of any organizations to which you belong. Ask them if they're interested in "trading horses" and suggest ways in which you can both benefit from each other's services.

#128 Service Corps. Of Retired Executives (SCORE)

The U.S. Small Business Administration (SBA) offers a free and very useful service to businesses, particularly early-stage businesses, through the Service Corps. Of Retired Executives, or SCORE.

SCORE consists of retired executives with valuable experience and insight. They've been through the wars before, had their share of successes and struggles, and can help to guide you through their experiences.

The organization typically has offices in every major metropolitan city in the U.S. as well as many smaller, regional offices. You can find SCORE offices through links to SCORE through the U.S. SBA web site located at www.sba.gov.

SCORE staff will not tell you what to do. It's your business. They make suggestions for things like where to look for financing, strengths and weaknesses of your business plan, operational considerations, staffing concerns, etc. They are not free staff members for your company. They are experienced individuals who can lend insight to help guide you to the most efficient successes. Use SCORE as a sounding board – a sanity check, if you will. Everyone should have access to experience (mentors) to help guide them.

Time Management

We must use time as a tool, not as a crutch.
John F. Kennedy

#129 Six Ways to Manage Time

1. Focus on your goals rather than on your tasks. Keeping the big picture in mind reduces stress and helps provide clarity when prioritizing tasks as they relate to the overall goal.

2. Have a notepad where you can jot down ideas that would otherwise distract you from the task at-hand. You can refer to your notes later when you have the time.

3. Work from "to do" lists. Having a list not only helps you remember what needs to be done, it also provides motivation for completing tasks and removing them from the list.

4. Work on *your* schedule. You know your inner clock better than anyone, your low times, and your high times. Organize your tasks based on level of effort or mental clarity required and complete high-energy or high-concentration tasks during the period of day you are most energized and concentrated.

5. Disorganization is a huge time-sucking factor. Remain neat, organized, and goal-oriented – not focused on single tasks.

6. Practice self-discipline. Learn to say no to others and to the procrastinator in you.

#130 Common Time Management Mistakes

Time management isn't about working *more*. It's about working more efficiently. There are several common mistakes we all make when it comes to wasting time and managing it efficiently.

One of the most popular time-wasting mistakes we make is jumping into our day or week without a list of tasks or goal in mind. It's impossible to measure how well you're making use of your time without any identified tasks or goals with which success can be measured. Always begin with a prioritized list and follow it.

Another overlooked mistake that we often make is trying to be productive in cluttered areas. You can't expect to be efficient or get much done if you're spending most of your time moving piles from one side of your desk to another or searching for memos you need to complete a task. Clutter not only gets in your way physically, it also blocks you mentally. At some point you'll become distracted and start feeling overwhelmed by the reminders of other tasks you've yet to do.

Lastly, as we run out of time we often do the one thing that slows us down most: steal more time from activities that energize us. We choose to sleep less or eat quicker or neglect workouts in favor of finishing tasks. In reality, you need to take those breaks to keep up your mental energy as well as maintain good health. While snagging time from these personal activities will help finish short-term projects, in the long-term you're robbing yourself of greater periods of time that you'll end up spending in bed trying to get over a virus you contracted while running your immune system down. Be good to yourself and keep the big picture in mind.

#131 Putting a Value on Your Time
Your time is valuable. Time is money. Don't waste time. You've heard it and probably said it before. There's a truth to it, particularly as an entrepreneur striving to grow and succeed. It's so important, particularly when you're small and trying to be larger, to make maximum efficient use of your time.

One way of looking at your time is to put a relative value on it. Ask yourself certain questions before diving into a task that may take up significant or important time. For example, are you better off taking care of your own accounting, such as entering and paying bills, running payroll, and reconciling your books? Should you instead bring on a part-time accountant or assistant to take care of these tasks while you focus on other important parts of your business, such as tasks specific to your growth? How much are you spending having yourself do these tasks at the expense of having other crucial tasks sit idle?

Another example involves taking on and doing project work. After you have been awarded a job, are you better off doing the work yourself or having someone else come on to do the work while you continue to look for other jobs? How valuable is your time as it relates to growing your business?

You can usually put a direct dollar value on your time and compare it to bringing on help in the form of employees or consultants. There is inherent risk when you add people, and perhaps your profit margin for that particular job may be less. However, when you consistently put a value on your time, the answers regarding how to address these issues typically are more obvious.

#132 Leveraging Your Time

Leveraging time will continually be one of the most important things you will do in your professional life. More and more information is being put in front of you everyday – when you're watching TV, listening to the radio, browsing the Internet, or dealing with day-to-day operations within your office.

Many things will help you to effectively leverage your time. An able assistant, effective and efficient verbal and written communication skills, and having procedures, around which you run your business and even your life, will all help with time management.

To do these things, other factors play a role, including rest, exercise, and diet, which provide more regular energy for addressing the multiple issues that will be presented to you each day. Managing stress will eliminate factors that may take productive time away from tasks.

Also, if you are fast on the keyboard or with reading, you can save enormous amounts of time. Think about the amount of time you spend typing e-mails and reading each day. The faster you're able to do each, while retaining accuracy and retention, the more efficient you will be.

#133 Entrepreneurial Organization
You have most likely seen traditional organization charts, showing a hierarchy that has leadership, assistants, and workers represented. It shows who is presumably in charge, reporting lines, and sometimes has a title associated with each person. That is tradition. People like to know where they are in the big picture.

In a truly entrepreneurial organization, traditional org charts don't represent what really goes on. Entrepreneurial organizations empower individuals to act in an entrepreneurial way, all for the good of the company. Traditional reporting lines are less relevant, as people work together – challenging each other, questioning each other, and cooperating – to reach the mutual goals of the organization.

True leaders and entrepreneurs are less concerned with who they are leading, how many employees they have, and having their names at the top of an org chart than they are with having their organization succeed. Empowering individuals to act in entrepreneurial ways engages everyone in reaching for success.

#134 Multitasking/Managing Multiple Priorities
It is amazing how increasingly important multitasking and effectively managing multiple priorities has become. Imagine, you're in your office, talking on the phone, checking your e-mail, reading news, and answering someone's question – all at the same time. How do you manage it all?

Organization is key. Keeping a list of your tasks – your "to do" list – isn't enough. The list needs to be prioritized, complete with due dates. You should have short- and long-term goals, and certainly don't lose sight of your long-term goals. However, your daily planning is critical to working through every task over time to get to reach your long-term goals. A good habit to get into in this regard is to ask yourself if the task you are about to perform is the best use of your time. Work on those tasks most important, not necessarily those that appear to be most urgent. Again: work on the important, not the urgent.

With multitasking can come stress – managing that stress is very important. There's seemingly so much to do and so little time to do it. Ask people how things are going, and most of them will say "busy." Don't focus so much on how busy you are. Take care of yourself, get plenty of rest and exercise, watch your diet, and work through your tasks in a systematic manner. Being well organized is the key.

#135 Save Time On-line
The Internet has grown to be a remarkable resource. In most cases, simply put, the Internet knows. What used to involve time to research and find answers to questions now can take minutes or even seconds thanks to on-line search engines with sophisticated inquiry capabilities.

Using the analogy that time is money, save time by finding what you're looking for on-line. Information about markets, products, companies, and more is readily available and rapidly accessible, making you more efficient.

Further, communications are also more rapid and timely thanks to e-mail and workgroups, and in a real-time sense, chat. You can reach multiple people multiple times daily, if needed, through on-line communication tools, allowing you to save time and work more efficiently.

101

Finally, other daily information, whether it's market information or news (daily information to supplement or support your efforts) is generally all available on-line and updated often, keeping you as up-to-date as you need to be, all in a timely manner.

#136 To Meet or Not to Meet
Not all leads are good candidates for face-to-face meetings or spending any time on at all for that matter. You can save yourself a lot of time and money by learning more about prospective customers and pre-qualifying them before setting up an initial meeting.

To limit the amount of time you waste on unqualified leads, learn enough about the prospective customer to answer the following questions:

- Does the prospect seem too difficult to work with?
- Can the prospect afford your products or services?
- Does the prospect have a problem that you can't solve?

Many businesses close sales on 90% of face-to-face meetings, but it's a time-intensive sales strategy. Once you've qualified a lead, though, chances of closing a sale and lessening time wasted are much better.

Marketing & Advertising

I think there is a world market for maybe five computers.
Thomas Watson, Chairman of IBM, 1943

#137 What Is Marketing?

Marketing is non-stop communication between your business and prospective and current clients. Whether you're providing a free workshop for the community and making them aware of your services or you're placing an ad in an industry publication, you're reaching out to prospective or current clients and making them aware of your products and services. More than that – you're making them aware of the benefits they will gain through purchasing your products or services.

Marketing encompasses both low-budget activities (such as writing thank you cards) and complete branded campaigns (such as visually similar billboards, brochures, and web site). As such, it can be a minimal- or extremely high-risk effort that may result in a few sales or a significant increase in clientele and revenue. Because of this, most entrepreneurs hate the idea of marketing. Fear of taking a risk and failing keep most business owners from marketing in the first place. This is detrimental to the health of the company because it's the fuel that keeps sales growing.

Marketing never ends. A good marketing effort begins with a plan, researching your target audience, and learning how to reach that audience. If you've identified these things properly and your product or service offers a needed benefit, your business will almost sell itself. You'll just need to take a leap of faith and invest some time and money in making your products and services known to the right buyers.

#138 What is Viral Marketing?

Viral marketing is a strategy that promotes the spread of your message, encouraging word of mouth advertising and resulting in exponential growth through exposure and influence. The message multiplies rapidly – much like a virus.

What makes viral marketing so successful is that it gives

great return on little investment. Offering highly effective and proven results, viral marketing leverages existing communication networks and requires low investment of energy and money.

An effective viral marketing message can be easily relayed and understand by others. You can benefit from exposure to unknown audiences and gain instant credibility through referrals if your message is easily understood and effortless to pass on.

Hotmail.com is a great example of a proven viral marketing strategy. First, they offer their product for free – good way to reel in prospective customers! Second, on each piece of outgoing mail, their tagline appears with an invitation to the recipient encouraging him or her to get a free Hotmail account of their own. This strategy allows Hotmail's customers to inadvertently (and of course effortlessly) market Hotmail with each outgoing mail that is sent. Hotmail.com took advantage of the unknown audience and instant credibility gained through receiving the offer from someone known instead of from Hotmail itself.

Remember the keys to any viral marketing strategy:

- Expect to expend energy.

- Make it easily understood and effortlessly conveyed to others.

- Offer something for free or a reason for passing the message along.

- Exploit common motivations and behaviors (fear, desire to succeed or be wealthy, etc.)

- As with any marketing campaign, immediately follow up with any leads that result from the effort!

#139 What is Guerrilla Marketing?

Guerrilla marketing, made popular by author Jay Conrad Levinson, is a term used to describe the achievement of conventional marketing goals using unconventional marketing methods. While that seems like a pretty broad definition, there are several definitive characteristics that help to define guerrilla marketing and its success.

When compared to more traditional marketing strategies, the most noticeable difference between guerrilla marketing and conventional marketing is that guerrilla marketing requires more investment of time than money. After all, to be unconventional takes creativity and time!

Guerrilla marketing tactics are outrageously inexpensive and great for small cash-starved businesses that have resources like time and staff but little money.

Your goal as a guerrilla marketer is to embed your business, your product, and your services in the minds of your prospective customers through innovative and inexpensive tactics. From handwritten birthday cards to pre-printed Rolodex⌣ cards, you can provide your prospects with free tools that will help them to remember who you are and what you have to offer.

For more information about guerrilla marketing, view the list of resources at the back of this book or visit www.jayconradlevinson.com.

#140 Develop a Marketing Plan

At its most basic description a marketing plan is a map that describes where your business is today, where you want your business to go, and how you plan to get your business there. It's important when developing your plan that you remember that planning is about the results – not the marketing plan itself.

There are six core components of a marketing plan including an executive summary, situational analysis, marketing objectives, sales forecast, expense budget, and a specific action plan.

1. *Executive Summary*
   Within the executive summary portion of your marketing plan, you should introduce your company and briefly highlight the main points of your plan.

   Include:
   - Description of the nature of your business and products and/or services you offer.

   - Length of time you've been in business and length of time your business has been at its current location.

   - Description of business activities including sales and customers, accomplishments and successes.

   - Description of your founding philosophy including mission statement and company objectives.

   - Description of your qualifications and the qualifications of key personnel. Include resumes in a section of your plan for supporting documents.

   - Description of your management team including salary information, ownership, board of directors, and organizational structure.

   - Closing statement outlining the main marketing objectives and strategies contained within the plan.

2. *Situational Analysis*
   A situational analysis includes information that provides an evaluation of your overall market and industry and how you compare with your competitors. In outlining the current state of your business and your industry, you'll want to do a lot of research including consumer analysis, competitor analysis, and market environment analysis. You should also conduct an internal SWOT (strengths, weaknesses, opportunities, and threats) analysis.

   Examine your product or service within the context of pertinent past, present, and future conditions. Leverage your business strengths and use them to develop strategies as they relate to the future conditions of your situation.

   It's important that you are realistic and honest when summarizing research findings and avoid bias.

3. *Marketing Objectives*
   Good marketing plans outline a business' objectives and relate those objectives to sales, market positioning, share, corporate identity, and consumer awareness.

   All objectives should be able to be implemented and measurable. A key sign that an objective is not likely to be implemented is if it can't be measured, tracked, or evaluated. It's essential that you can analyze all objectives.

   You can base your objectives on sales revenue, market share, or even specific marketing actions such as seminars or advertisements.

   While sales revenue is easy to track, some of your objectives may not be so easily measured such as market share or corporate identity. For this reason, when including your objectives you should also include their method of measurement as part of the objective itself.

4. *Sales Forecast*
   The sales forecast should show projected sales for all products and services. If you use a variety of methods to forecast sales, be sure to include a consolidated report of all of the forecasts you have made.

   You should include forecasts as they relate to specific plans of action. For example, if you intend to implement a direct mail campaign, you'll want to forecast sales that are driven by the development of your mailing list and number of mailings you do. As another example, if you implement distribution channels, you'll want to include a forecast of sales projections by marketing and distribution channels.

   Other methods of forecasting include projecting sales based on growth rate, market share, or predicting the number of units of each product or service you will sell at specified periods and the projected price per unit you expect to charge.

   Again, it's important that you are realistic with your forecasting and not too optimistic or pessimistic.

5. *Expense Budget*
   Your expense budget should include enough detail for expenses to be tracked month-by-month and provide you with the ability to frequently compare your plan to your actual results so that you can make necessary changes earlier rather than later.

   Most expense budgets of marketing plans also include a description of specific sales techniques, management responsibilities, promotion, and other elements.

6. *Specific Action Plan*
This section of your marketing plan is your opportunity to describe your specific plan and strategies for meeting your objectives. A marketing plan is measured by the results it produces; therefore, implementation of your plan is much more important than the ideas contained within it.

Good implementation requires a solid action plan that contains specific, measurable, and concrete initiatives that you can track and analyze.

These six core components described above are the bare necessities of a marketing plan. You can use this as a foundation for your business' marketing plan and build upon it as you see necessary.

#141 Five Marketing Mistakes to Avoid

1. *Lack of Product/Service Market Research and Testing.*
You can't expect your business' product or service to sell without understanding your market and prospective customers. Marketing requires knowing your competition, your prospective customers' motivation to buy, and industry trends. Without this knowledge, you'll be marketing blindly and won't be able to understand why you get the results you do.

2. *Neglecting to Make Doing Business with You Easy.*
   If prospective customers have to go out of their way to do business with you, growing your clientele will be a challenge. Good marketing makes it easy for prospective clients to learn more about your business' products or services, to contact you, and to purchase from you. As an example, any marketing pieces designed to encourage a prospective customer to purchase a product should include a phone number or reply card – something that makes it easy for them to place the order. Visitors to your web site shouldn't have to search for contact information either. Make it easy to do business with you.

3. *Neglecting to Set the Stage for Repeat Business*
   In addition to making it easy to do business with you for the first time, you need to make it even easier for customers to repeatedly come to you for solutions to their future needs. This requires great customer service the first time you serve them, constant communication, soliciting feedback, and remembering that they have additional needs you could potentially satisfy. Stay in the forefront of your customers' minds as a solution provider and they'll be loyal.

4. *Don't Change Your Marketing Message if it's Working!*
   Most entrepreneurs who tire of their own marketing campaigns think it's healthy to change their message from time to time. Don't make this mistake! If it's not broken don't fix it. What seems like "old" to you is what's needed to create repetition and branding of your business.

5. *Fragmented Marketing*
    Investing a few dollars here and a few dollars there may seem less risky than allotting your marketing money to a few venues, but that's not the case. Fragmenting your marketing is actually more damaging than protective. Instead of splitting your marketing dollars into small amounts and putting some towards billboards, some towards one publication, and some towards direct mail for example, invest a good majority in making one or two marketing venues the most effective they can be. In other words, spend your money on quality instead of quantity and you'll see a more effective return on your investment.

#142 Budgeting for Marketing
Financial:
Determine a percentage of gross income to spend annually on marketing. Set goals based on this budget and identify the actions required to achieve the goals. Don't forget to estimate the expenditures needed to carry out these actions.

Review the return on investment quarterly. Track, measure, and refine.

Time & Resources:
Be prepared to support the new clientele that results from marketing. Account for the resources and time that may be spent by your staff as customers respond to your marketing efforts.

#143 Finding Time for Marketing

For many small organizations, finding time for marketing can be challenging!

Here are some helpful tips for making effective use of the little time that you have and finding more time for marketing:

- Create a portable marketing projects folder or use a small notepad and carry it around with you to jot down marketing ideas when you're spending time waiting for appointments or sitting idle. A few minutes of notes can add up to hours of great marketing ideas.

- Instead of watching television or partaking in other unproductive tasks, spend that time writing sales letters, updating your web site, or writing e-mails to current and prospective clients.

- Carry industry magazines or newsletters with you or keep them in places you usually sit idle. Keep up with industry news and scan the publications for competitors' advertisements.

- When you're sitting back relaxing with the local newspaper, keep your eyes out for familiar names of clients, prospective clients, and partners. Send sympathy cards to people you know who are relatives of those in the obituaries. Send congratulatory notes and a copy of the article to those who were highlighted for their success. Let them know you're paying attention to what's going on in their life.

- Give clients just a little more than they ask for. A little more time. A little more attention. A little more of the product. A little more of the service.

- Give free advice or product expertise at networking functions. Make it part of your conversation at little league games, holiday parties, and other functions.

#144 Naming Your Business
When it comes to first impressions, you would be surprised how much impact the name of your business can have on a prospective customer's decision to buy.

Generally, when a need for your product or service arises, prospective customers more easily recall a business name that is short and memorable. It's also important that it differentiates you from your competitors. Using a name similar to a competitor won't help you build your clientele faster. It will only result in confusion.

If your business provides a specific product or service and you don't expect to branch out to offer other products or services, you might consider including the solution you offer as part of your business' name. It helps in marketing efforts when your business name conveys the product or service you offer.

Lastly, it's generally a good idea to not name your business after yourself. Not only can it damage your personal reputation if things do not go as planned and the business is not as successful as you hoped, but it can also raise some issues if you decide to pursue an acquisition and merger. More specifically, when another party is interested in acquiring your company, a business name that isn't tied to the owner is more attractive in the long-term vision of the company if the acquiring group has no intention of changing the business' name.

#145 Designing a Logo

Your business' logo is one of the most important pieces of your branding and marketing efforts. In fact, its often responsible for the first impression made. Therefore, it makes sense to say that you should put a great deal of thought into the design of your logo.

Some things to consider when coming up with a concept include your company's personality, your goals, the benefits you offer your clients, what differentiates you from your competition, and your audience's demographics and psychographics (or more specifically, their behaviors and motivations).

For example, if your clientele is youth you can get away with an unconventional and bold logo that makes your company appear energized and maybe even a little alternative. However, if your clientele is businesses and entrepreneurs, you're going to want to stick with colors that instill confidence and a more conservative look that reflects strength and stability.

It's highly recommended that you consider using a professional for the design of your logo. If you can't afford it, look to local colleges for design students who are looking for internships or better yet, look for ad agencies and media firms in smaller cities rather than metropolitan businesses that have to pay steeper rent bills and incur more costs that trickle down to their customers.

When you've come up with a design that you think reflects the majority of these characteristics, let it brand your organization. No matter how sick of your logo you may become, don't change it. Your customers and prospective customers aren't seeing it every day. And the times that they DO see it, you'll want them to recall having seen it before. That's the art of branding your business.

#146 Brand Your Business

View your organization from the eyes of your prospective customer. Are you being consistent with your message?

If you answer yes to any of the following statements, you may need to focus harder on branding your business in a way that increases awareness of your offerings and makes them clear and easily understood by prospective clients:

- Clients or prospective clients often tell me that they didn't realize we offer a particular service or product.

- When I attend local networking events, people often say that they haven't heard about my business.

- Prospective clients often get a little overwhelmed when I explain the numerous ways my business can help them. Or prospective clients don't seem to understand how my business' products can help them.

- Sometimes clients say that they didn't get the results they expected to get from my business' products or services.

Branding your business, its services, and its products with a message or identity that is easily remembered will help to increase customers' awareness of your offerings. It will also help to bring clarity to the client when they're looking for a particular solution that meets their needs.

A good company, product, or service message will state the benefits it offers to a client in a memorable and easily understood manner. Keeping your message consistent and in the forefront at all times will keep your offerings at the forefront of the minds of your prospective customers.

Business cards, letterheads, fax covers, brochures, web

sites, trade show material, direct mailings, advertisements, and even the message spoken when a company representative answers the phone should be consistent and clearly describe the benefits your business offers.

#147 The Rolodex® Card

One great way to make doing business with you easy is to provide a free Rolodex° card to prospective and current customers. You can purchase blank stationary that can be placed in your printer and create your own custom cards complete with logo and contact information.

Having your contact information at hand will make it convenient and easy for customers to do business with you without having to look up your business' number in the phone book.

Information to consider including on the card:

- Your name and title.
- Company mailing address.
- Your e-mail address.
- Your fax and telephone number.
- Your web site address.
- A brief description of the services and products you offer.

#148 The Power of a Memorable Phone Number

You're always working on ways to be memorable – your logo, meme, brochure, web site, and message. The power of a phone number, though, can enhance the effectiveness of people reaching you as well as their ability to stay in contact. It also shows to others that you took the time to be unique and make your number easy to remember.

Politicians sometimes use the year they're running for office, such as 555-2004. Others prefer to spell out something using the alphabetic equivalents on the phone, such as 800-HOLIDAY. Lastly, others prefer a catchy or memorably numeric combination, such as 800-800-8000.

Whatever you use, promote it. Make sure the number is in front of others. They're only going to know about the uniqueness of the number if they're told of it. You'll then be amazed how many people no longer have to look you up when they try and reach you. With as much information out there as people are trying to disseminate, an easy-to-remember phone number helps.

#149 The Importance of the Business Brochure
Some people still like to see it on paper. They want something tangible. They don't want to visit your web site. They don't want to put your demo CD into their computer. They don't use their computer for anything more than e-mail anyway. The business brochure remains an important way to demonstrate the quality and professionalism of your company.

Brochures are unlike other promotional media. On web sites, you can have hundreds of links to different pieces of information, making it a very interactive but periodically overwhelming information overload. Likewise, demo CDs or videos can be effective but they can also be either over-stimulating or cost-prohibitive. Brochures allow you to tell your story in one concise document, able to be touched, leafed through, and filed.

Many brochures try to say too much. They're so packed with information that the reader turns off. In brochure design, use an appropriate blend of imagery and text to tell your story. Use it as a way to show your capabilities without saying too much. People looking at a brochure are asking you for the time, not how the watch was made. The brochure should serve as a teaser to encourage the reader to want to learn more through direct contact with you.

#150 Produce and Distribute a Promotional CD-ROM

"Here's my brochure." Ok, if the brochure looks impressive, that can help with a client or potential client. "Visit our web site." That works, too, if they remember your web address and remember to visit the site. You're promoting yourself, and you're in a competitive world. How can you stand out? Create a CD that you can hand out or mail to prospects.

There are many advantages to producing a promotional CD, including:

- *Interactivity.*
  The user can control how they navigate through your information.

- *Motion.*
  Animation and video can enhance the attention paid to your information, increasing retention. Paper can't do this, and the web has some level of bandwidth restrictiveness.

- *Linkage.*
  Even from a CD, you can link to other promotional materials, such as your corporate web site.

- *CDs are substance.*
  Like brochures printed on glossy paper, a well-packaged CD or a CD in a non-standard shape can draw attention to it and remain a part of someone's library of materials.

Promotional CDs give you the ultimate opportunity to show off the capabilities of your organization. They combine the substance of paper with the interactivity of the web all while allowing you to use media such as animation, audio, and video, to enhance the users' experience.

#151 Business Signage 101

Signage can do wonders for small businesses. Not only does it help visitors find their way to your retail or office space, but it's a great form of advertisement – increasing awareness of your business to all in sight.

When one of our clients moved from a downtown location with no ability for signage to an area on the edge of town, they immediately made their presence known with signage off the interstate. The response was incredible. Although they had been in business for years, several people thought they were new to town and the "unknown company" generated a lot of buzz as people took notice of the signage.

Think of your business signage as outdoor advertisement. Include contact information for those who might pass by and wonder who you are and what you have to offer. You might consider including a one line description of your services or products, your web site address, and your telephone number.

There are several options when it comes to purchasing signage. You can buy vinyl adhesives for windows or purchase awnings for outdoors. Whatever you select, consider its purpose. Fewer companies are buying painted signs or foamcore because of their lack of durability. If you're looking for something to use indoors you won't have as much to worry about, but outdoor signage should be durable. Most outdoor advertisement companies will provide a warranty with their product, or at a bare minimum they'll let you know how long you can expect the sign to last.

Another important thing to consider when creating outdoor signage is readability. If your sign will be viewed from a distance, make sure you've considered font size and that it can be read easily from far away. A good exercise to help you ensure your sign is viewable from a distance is to take a scaled down version of the sign and print it on an 8 ½" by

11" sheet of paper. If you can read the text on the paper from 10 feet away, chances are your font will be large enough for others to view the larger sign from a distance. Of course, this is just a rule of thumb. If you're concerned, ask if the sign company can create a "proof" for you, or if they think there will be any readability issues. They are typically very helpful because they know that their business depends upon satisfied customers!

In addition to font issues, lighting can also affect readability. If your business is open during evening hours, make sure your sign is still visible!

Lastly, as part of an overall branding campaign, make sure to use a similar look as all of your other marketing material. Use the same fonts, the same colors, and incorporate your logo in your signage, too. Think of it as another weapon in your arsenal of marketing tools!

#152 The Client Referral Card
One of the most effective and least commonly used marketing tool is a client referral card. This is simply a business card that has your company's name, logo, and contact information on its face along with the names of a few of your clients who can testify to your fanatical customer service and solutions.

Offering a card like this tells your prospective customers that you have faith in your company's ability to serve and that you value the opinions of your customers.

Of course, you'll want to ask your clients if they mind if you use them as a referral before handing your cards out!

#153 When to Let Your Customers Do Your Job
It's a rare time when your customers will work for you instead of vice-versa! But one thing almost all satisfied customers are willing to do is refer you to someone else or offer a testimonial. This is a tremendous marketing and sales tool!

Customer testimonials that are specific about the results achieved are the most effective. When soliciting testimonials, ask your customers to be specific, including money they saved, or time they saved, as a result of using your services or products.

When your customers share positive feedback with you, ask them if you can use their feedback as a testimonial. Otherwise, solicit testimonials. If your clients don't have enough time to write a testimonial or they're not sure what to write, ask them if they would mind if you wrote one for them to review and sign.

The job of selling is much easier when you have a list of client testimonials – proof that you've done this before and you've done it well. Testimonials are success stories that help to build purchasing confidence in the minds of your prospective buyers.

#154 Creating Demand for Your Offering
Buyers don't put a sense of worth on your offering based on its intrinsic value. Your offering's worth is based on the demand for it. In order to supply something, you first need to create a demand for it.

Creating a demand requires:

- An on-going promotional strategy.

- Providing solutions to problems.

- Changing the way people do business and live.

- Generating requests for more information.

- Understanding the people you are selling or marketing to and how to appeal to them.

If creating a demand was about the quality of your product, how do you explain the popularity of some items such as pet rocks or silly putty?

#155 Introduction to Advertising

Just as it's important to hire an attorney to handle your legal matters, hiring a marketing and advertising firm is key to making the most of your promotional efforts. Experienced marketing professionals will take the time to research your industry and customer base and help you to identify the most effective way to reach your prospective clients and the most effective message to deliver to them to encourage them to purchase your products or services.

Whether you're advertising on your own or with the help of a professional, you'll want to become familiar with the types of results you can expect. It's important that you realize there is no reliable response rate that you can depend on. There is no solid way of calculating what kind of results you can expect based on how much effort and resources you invest. What you *can* count on is that results are tied to the message you deliver. Ads that speak to the needs of your prospective clients turn small companies into large companies. Your business' success really hinges on the message you attach to its name. Be believable. Differentiate yourself from your competitors. Focus on the benefits your products and services offer. Be consistent and repetitive.

Which media type should you use to reach your prospective clients once you have an effective message to deliver? Well, the answer depends on your message, your marketing budget, and your audience!

Outdoor Advertising

Outdoor advertising reaches the largest audience for your money than any other media, but your message is limited to eight words and an image. If your message is clear and your audience is mobile, this may be the wisest choice for growing consumer awareness.

Radio Advertising

Following behind outdoor advertising, radio advertising is next in line for reaching the largest audience for your money. The "con" of this media is that it's difficult to target geographically and can only be loosely targeted to specific demographics. If you're offering a service that includes delivery to the customer and doesn't require the customer to come to you, radio advertising could be an effective advertising tool for growing your business.

Cable Television

Unless you have the marketing budget that enables you to hire a professional, it's probably best not to use cable television as a form of advertising media because your ad will most likely appear "home-made" when compared to other larger companies who are using professional services. You'll have to weigh this con against the pros, though, and decide whether the advantages of moving images and spoken words and ease of geographical targeting outweigh the possibility of looking like a grassroots organization.

Newspapers

Newspapers reach an audience that is typically ready to make an immediate purchase. Although that is a great positive for using this type of advertising media, if the prospect isn't interested in your specific service at that exact moment, your ad is less likely to get noticed than it would in another type of advertisement media. Readers are reading to buy, not to become educated about services or products they weren't specifically looking for at that time.

Direct Mail

While it seems like the least complex way of advertising and offers highly targeted mailings, direct mail can be surprisingly expensive and requires having more than just a list of names and addresses if you're going to do it right! The costs involved with purchasing a mailing list of individuals most likely to purchase your products or services, and the cost of mailing to those individuals, can often exceed the budget of a small business. If you're looking for ways to implement a direct mailing without incurring the high costs, look for a like company who would be interested in co-marketing and splitting the costs of the mailing with your business. Both of you will benefit from the mailing, especially if your companies complement one another.

There are several other forms of advertising media that may fit your business better. We recommend that you talk with like businesses and an experienced marketing and advertising firm for recommendations specific to your business' target audience and industry.

#156 Five-step Effective Marketing Formula

Step 1: State the Benefits First
Within 15 seconds of reading your advertisement or listening to your presentation, convey to the prospective customer exactly what's in it for them – what you have to offer them.

Step 2: Establish a Sense of Urgency
Make it known to the prospective customer that they need to act quickly if they want to realize the benefits you have to offer.

Step 3: Describe the Offering
Once you have the prospect's attention and have established a sense of urgency you should describe the offering in detail.

Step 4: Tell Them What to Do to Get the Offer

Giving your prospective customer instructions on how to get your offering will help you to close the sale. Be specific. Do you want them to call your business? Should they mail in an order form? Or should they come in and mention the ad? Tell your prospect exactly what they should do to gain the benefits.

Step 5: Summarize

Once you've told the prospect what they need to do to get the offer summarize all five steps, reminding them of the benefits, establishing a sense of urgency, describing the offer and how to get it.

#157 Creating Effective Print Ads

There are several factors involved in creating effective print ads. While a glossy, well-designed marketing piece will get you noticed, the content (or copy) has to speak to your audience in order to get them to react in the way you want them to respond.

The first and foremost rule when creating content for your print ad is to speak to the motivations and behaviors of your prospective clients. What are their needs? What are their problems? What solutions can you offer them through purchasing your product or service?

The second rule in creating effective print ads is to keep it simple. Pick one message to convey and do it in a way that is quick and clear.

The third rule is to pick a format consistent with the types of ads your audience is used to reading. Nearly all advertisements are built on a structure that contains a headline, body copy or content, instructions, and more information about your company, product, or service.

Your headline should be short and clear and relate to your audience's needs while providing added value. Consider using something intriguing such as the word "free" or "innovative." For example, "Free Software Helps Increase Your Memory Ten-fold!"

The body of your ad should be easy to read and contain the important details your audience needs to know about your ability to solve their problems or satisfy their needs. For example, "Acme Incorporated's Memory Revival software has been proven to increase memory retention by 10 times in proven studies. Throw away those tedious organizers and give your secretary the day off. Now you can rely on your own memory to get the job done!"

The instructional portion of your advertisement should provide your audience with guidelines for taking advantage of your offer. Provide them with a telephone number and tell them to call now. Or provide them with a web site address and instruct them to visit the site to learn more. Most importantly, tell them what you want them to do and how to do it. For example, "Call 800-555-1212 for your free CD-ROM today!"

Lastly, your advertisement should provide contact and company information. Include your logo, web site address, phone number, address, fax number, e-mail address, or any other applicable information. A print ad wouldn't be effective at all if you didn't provide the information necessary for your audience to get in touch with you and make a purchase! After all, that's what advertising is all about.

#158 Stating the Offer Up-front

The most important thing to remember when writing a sales letter is to read it from the perspective of your customers. If you do this you'll realize that a sales letter that doesn't highlight the offer right at the beginning won't even get read. Recipients who realize you've sent them a sales letter but have to read half of the correspondence before finding out what's being offered will lose interest quickly! Always highlight the benefit to the customer within the first paragraph of your letter. Tell the recipient what it is that you are selling to him or her, explain the benefits gained from purchasing the offering, and tell the recipient what it costs.

This selling strategy applies to every form of advertisement including radio, television, and even voice mail messages you leave for prospective clients. Always state the offering and its benefits and costs up-front.

#159 Ten Benefits Your Prospective Clients Seek

1. More time gained.
2. Less time spent.
3. More money gained.
4. Less money spent.
5. More success gained.
6. Less failures committed.
7. More rewards.
8. Less work.
9. Free information, free products, free services.
10. A guarantee; worry-free purchasing.

#160 Co-operative Direct Mail

"Co-operative direct mail" is a highly effective way to advertise at a lower cost. There are a number of types of co-operative direct mail campaigns, but they all have one thing in common – shared cost. You split the fee of the production, packaging, and distribution of the mailing with other non-competitive businesses. Your advertisement is delivered as part of a grouped packaging of advertisements, reaching qualified, targeted audiences for a discounted cost.

Examples of co-operative direct mail campaigns include:

- Inserting promotional pieces with delivered orders.

- Inserting promotional pieces with invoices or account statements.

- Inserts bound in magazines such as subscription cards or business reply cards.

- Inserts in newspapers such as store fliers with coupons.

- Coupon booklets assembled from community merchants' advertisements.

Most programs have specific format, dimension, and weight requirements so be sure check into the details before creating and submitting your direct mail advertisements.

#161 All About Bulk Mailing
The United States Postal Service (USPS) offers reduced rates (sometimes more than 50% savings) for businesses that frequently do mass mailings. Bulk mailings of 50 to 500 pieces can be costly and you could benefit from the savings and demographic targeting bulk rate direct mailing services offers. The long-term savings and return on investment can be rewarding.

Businesses Bulk mailing isn't for every business, though. There is an annual fee and presorting requirement imposed on bulk mailings. If you're not active enough in your mailings, the costs could outweigh the benefits and you would be better off using regular mail services in place of bulk.

For more information about bulk mailing visit the USPS' web site at http://www.usps.gov.

#162 The Bumpy Envelope

With all the junk mail your prospective clients receive these days, how can you get them to open the mail you send? One quick and easy trick to getting your mail opened is to increase curiosity! Inserting a piece of candy or other marketing novelty (pens, erasers, buttons, etc.) to create a bumpy package is an effective way of peaking the recipient's curiosity and increasing the chances of your mail being opened.

#163 Trade show Dos and Don'ts

DO:

- Have a professional booth/area, preferably one that is easy to set up and tear down.

- Have friendly, knowledgeable people working in your area.

- Have useful information to provide to others, giving them something that will help them remember you and your discussion.

- Make the rounds and see others, including the competition.

DON'T:

- Don't have an overly cluttered booth/area.

- Don't spend too much time with one visitor. Politely ask to follow up with them later.

- Don't let your eyes wander when talking with a visitor. Focus on them.

#164 Frequent Buyer Programs

One key factor in good marketing is making repeat business easy for your existing customers. A good way to encourage your customers to remain loyal is by rewarding them for repeat business through implementing a frequent buyer program. Offer rewards such as discounts, novelties, tickets to events your business hosts, or other free incentives, simply for choosing your business.

#165 Gift Certificates

A gift certificate is one of the greatest referral tools you can use as part of your marketing efforts. What better way to grow your clientele than through the credibility established through the act of recommendation by those who give the gift certificates? It makes marketing easy when others pass them on to their friends or colleagues.

Offering gift certificates for the first time also gives you a good excuse to make contact with your existing customers and provide them with another great offer!

#166 Giving Free Samples

People love free stuff. It's human nature. Of course, it usually has to bring them some kind of value to be desired, but offering free stuff can help you increase awareness of your company and also build upon your list of prospects.

But don't just offer anything. Try to take advantage of the marketing opportunity and offer free items that promote your business. For example, you could offer free t-shirts that have your company web site's address on the back of them. Or you could offer a free industry report or newsletter that has your logo and contact information prominently displayed in the header or footer of the document.

Of course, there are very few *truly free* things in life. As such, people typically expect to give something in return so we recommend asking for the recipient's contact information. It's a great way to build upon your marketing contacts. At the same time, it's a good idea that you tell the recipient why you're collecting the information and what you plan to do with it. Otherwise, you'll end up with a list of contacts that simply wanted free stuff and have no interest in your services or products.

#167 Sponsoring or Hosting Contests & Sweepstakes
Similar to the fact that people are drawn in by the offer of free stuff, they're also attracted to the chance to win stuff.

Sponsoring or hosting contests and sweepstakes is a great way to run a cost-effective marketing campaign. It gets you exposure and helps you to gather information about your prospective customers. Sweepstakes and contests come in all forms. You can request participants to complete a survey for their chance to win. You can encourage them to refer a friend for a chance to win. You can even persuade them to make a purchase for a chance to win!

Whatever rules you create, the motivating factor to participate should achieve your goal of hosting or sponsoring the contest. If you're looking to build upon your mailing list of prospective or new customers, you'll want to request contestants' contact information and only permit first-time customers to enter.

If you're looking for a quick boost in sales or a contest that pays for itself, you'll want to limit the contest to paying customers. Keep in mind, however, that there are promotional rules you'll need to follow as a contest host. It's recommended that you look at other sweepstakes for examples and consult with a legal attorney and advisory board for input.

Sponsoring or hosting contests is a great way to spread the buzz about your company. You could even offer your products or services as the prize! The possibilities are endless. Be creative.

#168 Holding an Open House

When we want to sell our house, we invite others in. When our children want to show us how hard they've been working at school, we are invited to their class to see their projects. And when entrepreneurs want to earn the respect and awe of prospective clients, they hold an open house and invite all to come and see their office or retail space, meet their staff, meet other clients who provide instant credibility and act as referrals.

Holding an open house is a warm gesture and great way to establish trusting relationships with prospects. It's also an inexpensive marketing strategy that provides you with an opportunity to showcase your goods and services.

You don't need to be opening up a new location to host an open house. You can hold it concurrent with a holiday party or the anniversary of your company. Almost any excuse for an invitation to a group of clients and prospects to your place of business works!

#169 Donate Your Product or Service to a Charity

You can't always afford to give your product or service away, but in some cases, you can accomplish several good business goals at one time by doing so. Donations can help you to reach charitable goals you may have as a company, while at the same time creating an image locally or regionally as that of a giving organization.

Donating products or services to a charity can result in a positive press release about both the efforts of the charity and about your willingness to give to the cause. In some cases, this can result in other profitable work by making contacts with others involved in that charity.

#170 Continuous Marketing Strategy

Great entrepreneurs never let a day fly by without engaging in at least one marketing activity. Continuous marketing has effective results.

Many make the mistake of slowing down or stopping marketing efforts at their most profitable times. Because of the time it takes for customers to respond to your marketing efforts, any gaps in your marketing efforts will result in gaps in your sales results. Marketing continuously will help to maintain a constant revenue stream.

Tip: Continue marketing throughout the holiday season even when your customers may be on vacation because this is the period when your competitors WON'T be marketing.

#171 Tracking Marketing Results
If you can't track results how will you know which marketing, advertising, and/or promotional initiatives produce the best return on investment?

Always ask your client how he or she heard about your company, product, or service. Keep an electronic file containing this information, preferably a database or other document that can be sorted or searched.

For print promotional pieces such as advertising or direct mail, always include a "promo code" within the text of the advertisement. A promo code can be any number you include in an inconspicuous place on the advertisement and used for tracking purposes. When a prospective client responds to the advertisement, ask for the promo code so you can track the results of individual pieces.

To measure the success of your web site, ensure your web site host has an effective statistics tracker installed for your use. Be sure the tracker is not simply counting the number of times a page is refreshed and that it doesn't count the loading of page elements (such as graphics) as individual "hits." A good statistics package will track page hits or user counts by unique user "Internet protocol addresses." This kind of tracking tool will help to give a more accurate count of visitors and results by eliminating the tainted data that results from counting repeat visitors, page refreshing, or page elements. A simple page counter should never be used to measure the results and effectiveness of your web site.

#172 Measuring Return on Investment
Before you can measure the return on your investment in marketing efforts, you'll need to define success. Do you measure success by the number of clients you gain? Or by the number of products you sell? Or by the number of sales leads you receive? Define success and identify a unit of measurement for evaluating whether or not the investment you make in marketing can be perceived as worthwhile.

More often than not, you'll be comparing your specific predetermined goals to your results. For example, you may set a goal of gaining 100 new clients for this quarter and then compare that goal to your actual results. When you compare goals to actual results don't forget to account for intangible resources outside of money including time, personnel, and administrative work that's required for implementing your marketing strategies.

Regardless of how you define and measure success, it's important that you stay on top of it and also be sure to define *failure*. You'll need to be able to determine when a marketing effort simply isn't working for you and when to pull the plug and consider a new strategy.

#173 Become a Recognized Expert
You have areas of expertise – strengths that make you stand out. You use those strengths in your job, but it's possible that those strengths may not be recognized. Those strengths may not be positioning you as an expert in your field.

One of the best ways to become more recognized is to submit articles of interest to trade journals related to your field. Contact the magazine or journal to determine if they have a list of subjects of most interest to them, so that you can submit something with a greater chance to be considered. Publications get noticed both in the magazine or journal itself but also on your resume.

Another way to become recognized for your expertise is to present at conferences on topics specific to your strengths. You will be written up in the pre-conference publication, people will attend your presentation, and some will follow up with you after the presentation. Exposure is key, and you can create it yourself.

#174 Exposure through Writing Publications and Columns
One of the greatest ways to build consumer confidence and create awareness of your organization is to establish yourself as an expert in your industry. And one of the most cost-effective ways you can create such a presence is through writing publications and columns on topics in which your prospective customers are interested.

You can start small and create a free electronically distributed newsletter, or you can approach the dominant publications in your industry and submit articles for their consideration for inclusion. If you're planning on attempting the latter, contact the editorial group for the publication first and request an editorial calendar. Almost every publication operates based on an editorial calendar that details targeted topics for each month. Your article is more likely to be included if your topic relates to the publication's editorial agenda.

If you're successful and have an article published in a major industry publication, make photocopies of the article and distribute it to prospective and existing customers who might be interested in the article. Maximize your success!

#175 Writing Successful Magazine Articles
Successful magazine articles aren't only those that get published, but those that are of particular interest to the

readership. To be successful in writing an article for a magazine or journal, first do your homework.

Ask the editor, either via telephone or e-mail, if there are topics of particular relevance to the audience that they would like to see addressed. Also, read past copies of the magazine to get a feel for the type of articles that are written. Read letters to the editor to see which articles the readership found particularly interesting. Much can be learned from knowing as much about the magazine as possible before writing an article for it.

#176 How to Write a Press Release
There should be a consistency to the way you write press releases. Those publishers you submit the press release to look for a particular style and format when they consider a press release for print.

One of the easiest ways to learn how to write a press release is to see how others write them. Go to any large company's web site and look under a section specifically for news or press releases.

What you'll find as common elements to each press release includes:

- A location from which the news initiates.

- An executive summary describing the major components of the news.

- A body section providing more detail, in many cases including quotes from key players.

- A summary of the news with contact information for the company from which the news came.

#177 Putting Together a Press Kit
One of the best ways to ensure that your press release catches the attention of a reporter is to provide a press kit.

A press kit is a complete package that supports your press release and provides the editor with additional information from which they can build a complete story.

What should you include in your press kit? Below is a list of the basic information that should be provided with your press releases:

- Brief description of your organization including the names, titles, and *brief* bios of key personnel, the date the business was established, services and products your business offers, and contact information.

- Include up to three *related* press releases or articles that have been written about your organization and published.

- Photographs of products, corporate images, or key personnel related to the press release are helpful to the press. Include one vertical and one horizontal shot for layout purposes.

- Keep your information current.

- Get creative and get noticed. Include small, related items that will help get your article noticed. If your press release is about a new product you're offering and it's small enough to fit in the package include a sample. Otherwise, find something related to include and catch the press' attention.

Some press employees would rather receive some information and the option to request a press kit if they're interested. A fast growing trend is to offer a link to an on-line press kit that allows the reporter to download related information if they're interested.

Regardless of how you distribute your press kit, it is a valuable tool you'll want to make available to help boost your chances of having a release published or a story written about your company.

#178 Speaking to the Press

If you get the hang of speaking to the press and you can establish a few good relationships, their contacts and outreach can be extremely beneficial to the marketing of your organization.

If you've never spoken to the press before – it can be an intimidating task. Let us be the ones to tell you from experience that reporters are far too busy to help ease your anxiety, or extract the highlights of a story from you, before determining whether or not it's something worth writing about. It's YOUR job to sell your story. If you don't sound like you have faith in your own press release and can't present it in a manner that makes it sound like it's important news, how can you expect a news reporter to view it as such?

So, put your anxiety aside and focus on your story instead of your experience speaking with the press (or lack thereof). Before you make contact with any reporters or media personnel, practice your pitch. Mock interviews can be useful and may help to identify questions before they're asked. Be prepared to answer.

When you're ready to speak to the press be clear, honest, and to the point. Pay attention to your presentation and make eye contact with the reporter to establish credibility and trust.

Also, while it may be difficult – stay relaxed. Speak with confidence and you'll earn respect.
Remember if your story is rejected or not picked up by the press, don't let it get to you. The term "newsworthy" is subjective. What may not be of interest to one reporter could be another reporter's idea of a main feature.

Lastly, reporters are often running on deadlines and don't have much time to listen to your pitch. Always begin a conversation with asking if they have a minute to talk or if there's a better time for you to call. When they're ready to listen, make it quick and concise. They'll appreciate your understanding and will respect your courtesy.

Internet Marketing

When I took office, only high-energy physicists had ever heard of what is called the World Wide Web. Now, even my cat has its own page.
President Bill Clinton

#179 Banner Ads 101

'Banner ad' is the term given to most of the advertisements you typically find on web sites. More often than not, the advertiser is paying the owner of those web sites to display that banner. Fees can be based on the number of times the ad is clicked by visitors (cost per click or CPC), or the number of times the ad was viewed without clicking (cost per thousand impressions or CPM). If the banner ad space has a CPM of $20, it costs the advertiser $20 for every 1,000 impressions (or times it is viewed). If the banner ad space has a CPC of $20, the advertiser pays $20 each time the advertisement is clicked on by a viewer but no fees are charged for simply displaying the image.

To assess whether or not your banner ad is effective, you should calculate the "Click Through Ratio" (CTR) by dividing the number of times your advertisement was clicked on by the number of times it was viewed. For example, if your ad was viewed 1,000 times and received 20 clicks, the CTR would be 20:1000. This means 2% of the 1,000 impressions led to click through traffic.

#180 Creating Banner Ads

Banner ads can be an effective way of getting traffic to your web site and boosting your on-line sales or consumer awareness. While you can use just about any kind of graphics software or free banner generating tool on the web to create your banner ad, serious thought should be put into the design of the ad itself.

The typical dimensions of a banner ad are 468 pixels wide by 60 pixels in height, but check with the webmasters of the sites that will host your banner ad to find out what dimensions they require. They may also have a file size limit around 10-20kilobytes. Most limit you to this kind of small file size to save download time for the users. After all, how can you expect for a user to click on your banner ad if they don't wait around long enough for it to download and display?

There are a few tips to remember when trying to keep your banner ad under the file size requirement. First, use fewer colors. The more colors you integrate the larger the file size will become. Always optimize your graphic when you save it. If you're saving it as a JPEG/JPG file, save it as medium quality instead of high if you can do so without sacrificing its appearance. If you're saving it as a GIF file, try adjusting the number of colors used and limiting the palette to only a few.

With requirements in mind, you should focus on ensuring your banner ad is effective by:

- Avoiding creating transparent banner ads since you can't always predict what kind of background they will be placed upon and that could affect their appearance.

- Considering using an animated banner with 2 or 3 "frames" or changing pictures. Just be sure the file size requirements are still met. Also, make sure you leave enough time between animations for the viewer to read any text in your banner.

- Avoiding tricking users into clicking on your banner by making it appear like a user interface such as a form submission button or checkbox. It's generally discouraged and often leaves the user *feeling* tricked. Plus, it's not cost-effective if you're paying for each click you *tricked* out of a user instead of genuinely interested consumers!

#181 Link Partnerships
As the World Wide Web increases in population the criteria for indexing of these web sites by search engines continuously evolves. One of the ways to help promote your web site and boost your listing in some of the search engines is to establish link partnerships with similar web sites.

Web sites that are frequently linked to from other sites are considered to be more popular and listed closer to the top of some of the search engines as a result.

Consider contacting similar businesses that offer like, but not competitive, products and services. Ask them if they would be interested in "cross-linking." Cross-linking is the term given to reciprocal links or a link partnership. This involves placing a link on your web site that points to the partner site in exchange for their linking to your site. Both web sites benefit from the advertisement and seemingly popularity.

#182 Understanding Search Engines
Without search engines the Internet wouldn't be one quarter as valuable as it is. Much like you probably can't find your way to the Changanmoon restaurant in Korea without a map, you'll never find their menu on the Internet without a search engine. Even *with* a search engine, there's no guarantee if you're not familiar with the way search engines work!

Three of the most popular search engines used today can be found at:

- www.google.com
- www.yahoo.com
- www.aol.com

There are some almost universal formatting "tricks" you can use with search engines, but for the most part, each engine functions a little differently. For instance, at About.com, the sites listed are hand-selected by Guides – humans they've hired to find some of the better topical resources for which most people search. Whereas other search engines index sites based on words within the web page content. Some search engines proactively crawl across the Internet indexing content – these are often called "spiders." Other search engines, like Yahoo, index their web sites under categories based upon the category selected by the person who submits the web site for indexing.

Although it's best to look at each search engine's advanced search options, here are some general tips that apply to most of the engines:

- To search for an entire phrase, word for word, enclose your query in quotation marks. Entering "Changamoon restaurant in Korea" will search for matches for that exact phrase. Whereas, if you entered that phrase without the quotations, the word "in" would most likely be eliminated and results for each of the other three words, independently, would be retrieved. This means that results may include the word "Changamoon" and not "restaurant" or "Korea."

- If you want to eliminate any results that contain a specific word, you can do so by including them and prefacing them with a hyphen. For example, if you know there's also a restaurant called Changamoon in Florida, you can eliminate any results that contain the word Florida by entering the following query: *Changamoon restaurant Korea -Florida.*

- You can also use the word "OR" in your query to look for results that contain one word or another. For example, if you want to look for sites related to Florida's or Korean's Changamoon restaurant you could enter the following query: Changamoon restaurant Florida OR Korea.

- Of course, you can combine all of the above to create very specific searches. If you aren't getting the results you want, think about the words you've chosen and try and think of alternate, more frequently used, words. For example, *"dining"* may be a better option than *"restaurant."* Sometimes less restrictive searches have better results. For example, *"Changamoon"* may have been the best query in the example above if it's not a common name for a restaurant.

To learn more about how others search for information on the Internet, check out www.searchenginewatch.com. This site shows you the most popular queries and provides a wealth of information on finding information on the World Wide Web.

#183 The Digital Signature
Don't underestimate the power of the digital signature! The signature file, which can be added to e-mails you send to prospective clients, is an excellent marketing tool. Almost all of the popular e-mail programs, such as Microsoft® Outlook Express or Eudora®, have this feature allowing you to automatically sign all out-going correspondence, branding every e-mail with your business' contact information.

On a side note, make sure you aren't branding personal e-mail with professional information. You could get yourself into some trouble! We're reminded of a woman (whose name we'll keep anonymous to spare her from the embarrassment) who had a tendency to forward jokes and urban legends. One particular e-mail she forwarded was an urban legend about a fictitious act that was conducted by a disgruntled employee at a popular restaurant. The restaurant hired Pinkerton Detective Agency to trace the e-mail back to its origin. Needless to say, she received a phone call one morning after the Agency followed a trail of e-mails that had her digital signature pasted at the bottom. No word of a lie – it happened. Take caution and be careful what you're putting your name on.

Include your business' contact and branding information in your signature such as:

- Your name and title.

- Your business' name.

- Your business' meme, slogan, or tagline if one exists.

- Your business' phone number, fax number, and web site address.

When your digital signature is included in your out-going e-mail, it's quite possible that more people than the recipient will see it. Often, people forward useful information to other users without deleting the digital signature of the original sender.

#184 E-commerce 101
In the midst of all its hype, it's important to recognize that a web-based storefront is not suitable for every business or industry. If your primary business involves selling weight-lifting equipment or large engines, chances are the shipping costs you or your customers would incur would completely discourage sales if the customer can pick up a similar product at a local business.

E-commerce works best for product-oriented companies with innovative, specialty, and hard-to-find items. It's perfect for wholesale-direct companies and other businesses that can compete with the multitude of e-commerce businesses that are fighting for the business of the client who is searching for the lowest price. There are so many tools for consumers on the web to help them find the lowest price, the best shipping rates, the closest dealer, and other factors to consider when making a purchase that competition can be fierce.

If you're wondering if e-commerce is for you, rather than jumping right into the costs of setting up a secure store to take in and process credit card orders, test your product by establishing distribution relationships with existing e-commerce sites or listing your products on auction sites such as e-Bay. This will help you to determine whether or not there is a demand for your product before incurring the costs associated with doing business on the World Wide Web.

If you've done the research and you're ready to set up your virtual shop, there are many things to consider. To avoid legal and security issues, you should consult with a professional web site design and Internet marketing firm.

There are many options available to a small business wishing to reap the benefits of a new market such as the Internet. You can set up shop with some of the existing hosts such as "Yahoo!" or "Powerful Hosting." For a flat monthly rate plus $X per product you can create your store on-line. Most providers charge a "per transaction rate." This is in addition to a percentage of sales that is taken by your merchant account provider. You'll need to price your products wisely to ensure you're profiting! Read the fine lines and thoroughly research your options.

The most profitable way to do business on-line is to hire a professional firm who is willing to create your e-commerce site for a one-time fee without any per sales transaction fees. The costs up-front may be significant, but if you've done your research and you know there's a market on-line and a need for your service, the long-term revenue generated will far outweigh the costs of the initial set up.

It may be difficult to find a consultant who is flexible with their terms, but always negotiate when you're selecting a firm. They have room to bend – at least a little. However, realistically you should expect to spend between $2,000 – $10,000 depending on the types of options you want such as order processing, e-mail confirmations, live credit card processing, etc. Of course, these rates vary based on complexity of the project and the geographic location of the firm you hire. Generally, firms located in smaller towns are more affordable.

Another way to save on costs is to forgo live credit card processing. The term "live credit card processing" refers to the ability to process the customer's order and charge the card all within your application without the need for a terminal or a phone call to approve the transaction. If you create a shopping cart system that simply collects information securely about the customer's order and groups it all together for your viewing, then you manually enter the credit card information in a terminal, you can save yourself a lot of extra costs. Especially if you already have a terminal set up for your business offline.

A final word of caution regarding e-commerce . . . never encourage your customers to send their credit card information via e-mail. Never collect their credit card information in an insecure environment. Always encrypt your customers' information. Encryption is basically scrambling and encoding the information in a way that makes it unreadable to others. And always require user names and passwords to areas that contain sensitive data. To learn more about security, consult a professional.

#185 Ten Reasons to Have a Web Site

1. Compete for and serve the customers your on-line competitors are serving.

2. Increase your clientele through reaching a global audience.

3. Provide product information, directions, and contact information to those consumers who research on-line before purchasing.

4. Network virtually.

5. Release time-sensitive information.

6. Generate product sales revenue at half the administrative costs.

7. Offer 24-hour service.

8. Solicit feedback from web site visitors.

9. Test market new products and services without all the expense.

10. Demonstrate your product.

#186 The Power of a Domain Name

The URL address, or domain name, of your web site is almost as important as the name of your business when it comes to e-commerce and having an Internet presence. Your domain name should be carefully selected.

When you're selecting a domain name for your business' web site, consider your visitors and consider your corporation's identity. Your domain name should be:

- *Representative of your company*
  Domain names that reflect your business' name, service, product, or benefits are easiest to recall and find during web searches.

- *Memorable*
  Rhymes, short catchy phrases, or acronyms are another option if you can't find a domain name similar to your business' profile.

- *Short and simple*
  Try to avoid hyphens or lengthy names. They're fine as a last resort.

- *Free from confusion when spoken*
  You should pick a domain name that doesn't require reading to be remembered by a prospective customer. For example, www.icuatwork.com and www.iseeyouatwork.com can't be differentiated without explanation when spoken.

- *.Com vs. .Net vs. .Org vs. .Biz, etc.*
  Generally, if you're a for-profit business, it's best to find a domain name with the ".com" extension since that's the extension with which most people are familiar. Non-profit groups should use the ".org" extension. ".Net" was originally intended for Internet technology companies such as Internet service providers, web site designers, and other Internet businesses.

  A domain name is an important element in your branding campaign. Choose wisely.

#187 Creating a "Sticky" Web Site

When used to describe a web site, the term "sticky" refers to a site that is able to get viewers to stay at the site longer and come back frequently. Sticky web sites are more likely to turn viewers into customers.

10 Ways to Make Your Web Site "Sticky"

1. Keep content fresh! Feed daily news or update the site frequently with new information.

2. Use appropriate interactive tools for feedback and user participation such as chat rooms, discussion boards, polls and surveys, or feedback forms.

3. Teach your viewers. Adding tutorials and quick how-to articles to your site is a great way to bring viewers back. Proving you're an expert in your field will also help turn viewers into customers.

4. Offer an electronic newsletter. Allow viewers to subscribe to your "e-newsletter" and include advertisements or descriptions of your new products and services in the newsletter.

5. Keep your web site pages light in content. In other words, don't fill the screen with a lot of text and expect your viewers to stick around!

6. Make the navigation intuitive. Use familiar navigation tools such as hyperlinks, buttons, or pull-down menus. Ask others to navigate your site and give you feedback. Better still, make it possible for viewers to provide feedback when they're not able to find what they're looking for.

7. Give something away for free and hold a contest that allows viewers to enter daily! What better prize to give away than your products or services?

8. Brand your web site with your corporate identity. Make sure your logo is on the site and visible to the viewer. Displaying the web site's address on the page along with your organization's contact information will help them find their way back to you.

9. Provide value-add information to your viewers. This could include recommended books, tips, top tens, product manuals, tools for download, or other useful information.

10. Make your site visually appealing and easy to read. Dark text on a light background is more apt to keep your viewers reading. Keep the graphics to a minimum, though! Excessive use of graphics will force your pages to load slower and potentially turn your viewers away.

#188 Web Site Privacy Policies
According to a study by Forrester Research, 2 out of 3 e-commerce shoppers are concerned about privacy when purchasing on-line. Having a good privacy policy and making on-line consumers aware of it can help to settle their minds and encourage a purchase.

What should you include in your privacy policy? Inform users what kind of information you are collecting and why. Explain how the information will be used by your organization, and whether or not the information may be shared with others. Lastly, you should let users know of any choices they have if they want to use your site but don't want to share any information.

You can find examples of privacy policies on most of the larger sites such as CNN.com. Most privacy statements are found at the end of the page. Structuring your privacy policy similarly is a great way to start.

Privacy policies provide consumers with purchasing confidence and will encourage them to trust in your service.

#189 Tracking Your On-line Customers
There are several ways to track your web site visitor data. Some are quite basic, such as adding a "counter" to total the number of "hits" or views a web page receives. Other options are much more involved and will track data specific to each user.

You would probably be surprised by just how much information you can learn about each person that visits your web site. Some data is stored on their computer and can be retrieved if you're using the right tracking software. This includes information such as the address of the web page the user visited before coming to your site, which pages they viewed on your site, the type of web browser they're using, the type of operating system they're using, and how long they stayed viewing your site. All of this information is valuable to your marketing efforts. If 30 viewers read a product page and buy the product, yet 3,000 view another product and no purchases are made, it might say something about your product or about the information that's provided about that product.

You can also learn about your customers' activities, interests, and opinions through tracking where they have come from. This is also a good source for understanding how customers are learning about your site!

Never settle for a "counter," which often simply tracks how many times a single page is refreshed. This kind of information adds no value to your research. Look for a full web statistics package and learn what your customers want from your site so that you can better your on-line service.

#190 Ten Web Sites for Entrepreneurs & Small Businesses

1. www.fortune.com

2. www.workingsolo.com

3. www.entrepreneurmag.com

4. www.homebusinessmag.com

5. www.inc.com

6. www.entrepreneur.com

7. www.startupjournal.com

8. www.businessgrower.com

9. www.sba.gov

10. www.findlaw.com

Technology

Science can amuse and fascinate us all, but it is engineering that changes the world.
Isaac Asimov

#191 What Is an Intranet?

An Intranet is a private web-based network that connects a group of computers and allows for communication and collaboration between all. Computers on the network can create, share, and update files, share printers, and participate in real-time discussions. Intranets increase internal company efficiency.

If your company has 4 or more employees and requires constant communication and data sharing, you could benefit from the offerings of an Intranet. Locate a computer network consultant, describe your needs, and ask for the most affordable solution that will meet those needs. Be sure they don't sell you a Lexus if all you need is a bicycle. If you don't feel educated enough to understand your needs, ask owners of similar businesses and similar needs what kind of solution they have implemented. You can also learn the technical terms and gain a basic understanding of the components of an Intranet by visiting www.whatis.com.

#192 PC Productivity/Maintenance

Technology can make you efficient, organized, and productive. Technology can also stop you dead in your tracks particularly if you are extremely dependent on it. Getting the most out of technology, and perhaps most importantly, your personal computer can give you advantages over your competitors.

Productivity tools such as word processors, spreadsheets, and databases allow you to put your thoughts, plans, and data in organized places and organized formats. In doing so, you create many different files. You need to know and remember where they are, how to access them, what they do, and how they differ.

Naming conventions are important in finding what you're looking for, particularly when managing large numbers of files. Modern operating systems allow for longer file names. Use longer names to describe in as much detail as possible what the file contains. This will help you sort and find efficiently. Also, remember to <u>back up your files regularly</u> in case of computer malfunction or crash.

Managing all of these files involves creating, deleting, renaming, and moving files on a regular basis. Remember to perform basic maintenance tasks on a regular basis, including:

- Unused files should be backed up or deleted.

- Running disk cleanup and defragmenter should be done once every couple of weeks.

- Keeping up to date with Windows or Macintosh operating system updates, anti-virus updates, and other software updates will help your computer keep up with the ever-changing times.

Regular maintenance helps give your computer longer and more efficient life, making you more efficient and saving you money in the long run.

#193 E-mails

E-mail is a technological advancement allowing for new ways of communicating with everyone in your network – co-workers, employees, clients, potential clients, bankers, accountants, et al. There are many pros as well as some cons to be aware of when considering use of e-mail.

Initial contact through e-mail is generally non-intrusive, but it lacks the personal element. Follow-up thank you notes are good in e-mail if the recipient is an e-mail enthusiast. Sometimes a personal, hand-written note works better.

Be careful. Humor, sarcasm, and other emotions can be missed or misinterpreted in e-mail, at times doing the exact opposite of your intention. Also, unwanted e-mail, usually called "spam" is not only undesired by the recipient but also ineffective.

157

On the other hand, you can stay in touch with literally hundreds of people on a fairly regular basis by both writing and responding on your own schedule. The people you write to can reply when it's convenient to them, providing you with the polite persistence to stay in touch most effectively.

#194 Sending E-mail Attachments
Technology has made it possible for us to send and receive documents, images, presentations, and other media. We're no longer limited to mere text! But many of those who have used e-mail to send attachments haven't considered important things such as file types, file sizes, and other things that need to be factored in when using the technology.

The most common mistake people make when sending attachments is assuming that the recipient will be able to open the document. Not everyone has the same software, so be sure to check with the recipient to see if they can open your files before you send a document. When it comes to images, the most popular file types are .gif and .jpg files. Most people will be able to open those images. Other popular document file types include Microsoft Office's files (.doc, .xls, .ppt), Adobe Acrobat (.pdf), Hypertext Markup Language documents (.html, .htm), and other universal text formats (.txt, .rtf).

The second most common mistake people make when sending e-mail is assuming that the recipient will see it in the exact same format and appearance as it was sent. You know that beautiful stationary you use for the background? Or those embedded smiley faces or text formatting (bold, italic, etc.)? Forget them. More often than not, the recipient isn't using the same e-mail client software as you (Outlook, Outlook Express, Eudora, etc.) and the e-mail isn't read the same way it was written in terms of formatting. Some people prefer to read their e-mail as plain text, which means all images and formatting is stripped from the e-mail or included merely as an attachment. Don't rely on formatting and images to get your message across.

The third most common mistake people make (and possibly the most annoying) is not considering the size of the e-mail they're sending. Most business people are on the go and are checking their e-mail from regular dial-up accounts through a phone line in the airport or in the hotel. They can't afford to wait for the time it takes to receive a large e-mail. Although, on average, most people are capable of receiving files up to 2 MB at a time, it's generally not appreciated unless it's expected. If you have to send a file that's over 500K in size, ask the intended recipient ahead of time if it's a good time to send it.

#195 Faxes
Many think that faxes are becoming increasingly obsolete, with the advent of other technologies such as e-mail, chat, mobile phones, etc. However, faxes can be a very effective way of communicating with people in your network. Simply put some people prefer paper.

Several things help when sending faxes so that they are received and read including:

- A poor fax machine or poor fax paper can result in a hard-to-read fax on the recipient's end.

- Sending your fax in reverse order allows the fax to be received in order on the other end.

- Remember a cover page!

- Always include at least the recipient's name and your name and number in case the fax doesn't come through completely or there is another problem.

#196 Pagers

Pagers are one of the least expensive as well as least intrusive and most effective technologies for contacting someone or being contacted. They're not for everyone; particularly those who want or need instantaneous live contact with someone else.

Paging someone allows you to let him or her know that you want to make contact. You call, leave your contact number, and wait for them to find a time or place to get back to you. It's generally unknown to you when you'll hear back, if at all. There's no voice mail like on many mobile phones so you are, as the sender, unable to be specific.

If you are the one receiving the page, again, you will know who is trying to contact you. The hard part might be in finding a place to get back to the sender. That might be a good thing for you, particularly if you don't want to be immediately interrupted. Also, as mentioned earlier, pagers, even nationwide pagers, are generally less expensive than mobile phones.

Customer Relations

Business is not just doing deals; business is having great products, doing great engineering, and providing tremendous service to customers. Finally, business is a cobweb of human relationships. •
H. Ross Perot

#197 It's All About the Customer

Believe it or not. People don't want your products and services. What they DO want, however, is an answer to problems, a solution to needs, and ways to satisfy wants and desires.

Always focus on the benefits your business offers and your buyer's mind. Don't describe your business. Instead, describe the needs your business can satisfy.

Market using factors that motivate your customers. There are several basic motivating factors your customers use to make buying decisions including needs, wants, desires, and fears.

For example…
Wants: Razor companies don't sell razor blades. They sell the clean shave a man wants.

Needs: Diaper manufacturing companies don't sell diapers. They sell dry baby bottoms without rashes, leak-proof protection, and the ease of transition to toilet training.

Fears: Antiseptic manufacturers don't sell antiseptic products. They sell the freedom from worrying about infections, germs, and contaminated surfaces.

Desires: The state lottery doesn't sell lottery tickets. They sell the chance to be wealthy.

Focusing your marketing efforts on the motivating factors of potential buyers and expressing only the benefits your company offers will help to build your clientele and increase your market share and profits.

#198 Impressive Introductions

People being introduced don't always like to hear how great they are, but when it's done with class it can make for an impressive introduction. A significant introduction creates a situation where the person being introduced is immediately important in the eye of others. It can help to create the right kind of atmosphere for doing the type of business needing be done.

An impressive introduction includes detailing some of the more significant accomplishments of the person being introduced, particularly those relevant to others present. Introduce the person in a voice loud enough for all needing to hear to hear, but no louder. Engage everyone present by making eye contact with everyone, unless it's a large audience. You are presenting someone that you believe has importance to those who are present, and your confidence shows others that you have confidence in the person you're introducing.

#199 The Handshake
Most entrepreneurs realize that a handshake is important when making an impression. However, not many know when to shake or not shake, and how to effectively shake another's hand! There is no formal class or rules to follow – no handshake teacher or institute. But we do have several tips to mastering the art of handshaking.

When to shake another's hand…

- During introductions and re-introductions.

- When formalizing agreements.

- When a prospective client enters and leaves the room.

- When you enter and leave a room of prospective clients.

Effective First-time Handshaking Tips
Say your name and extend your hand at a slight angle with your thumb pointing upward. Your thumb joint should connect with the thumb joint of the person you're greeting. Once contact has been made, put your thumb down and

163

wrap your fingers around the underside of the other person's palm. Be firm with the shake, not limp, but don't squeeze too hard!

#200 Customer Service Essentials

If you're in a service-oriented business, there's nothing you can do that is more important than to take care of your clients. Tending to the business you have, particularly if your clients subscribe to your service, ensures your ongoing success. A few simple essentials when it comes to customer service include:

- Ask your customers what they need.

- Listen.

- Reply to customers' requests quickly.

- Go out of your way for your customers – do something special for them.

#201 Dos and Don'ts of Listening

DO:

- Listen attentively – focus on who is talking and give them your undivided attention.

- Listen well – being able to ask pertinent follow-up questions shows others that you were listening.

- Relate – be able to relate what's being said to things of relative importance.

DON'T:

- Doodle – doing something else while someone else is talking, other than taking notes, shows disrespect to who's talking.

- Nod incessantly – people who always nod in agreement can be taken as not really listening.

- Interrupt frequently – interruptions are sometimes appropriate, but give the person who's talking a valid chance to finish their thought.

#202 Remembering Your Current Customers

Just because you've earned the business of someone doesn't mean you're guaranteed that they'll come back to you for your services or products in the future – even if they were pleased the first time!

Never forget that your competitors are constantly marketing to your existing clientele. You need to give them a reason to return to you and not wander to your competitors and spend their money elsewhere.

Remember that the cost of keeping a client is much less than the cost of finding new ones. Let your current customers know that you appreciate their business, and offer them reasons to come back to you again. Consider offering current clients discounts on future services or products, or send appropriate seasonal greetings, or call them just to find out how they're doing and whether or not they are pleased with their relationship with your business.

Letting them know that their patronage is an important factor in the success of your business and that you're appreciative will keep them loyal and help to ensure follow-on business.

#203 Winning Your Clients with Humor

A good sense of humor, particularly with good timing, can be key to personalizing relationships with clients. Too much humor can show a lack of seriousness, but injecting humor in a timely manner relaxes sometimes-tense atmospheres and helps friendships bud.

Sarcastic humor has its place, but can sometimes portray negativity when what clients typically want is positivity. Sarcasm can also be misread if it's delivered wryly. Self-deprecating humor can be effective because it shows your clients that you can take a joke as easily as give one.

Finally, it's important that business is fun. It's part of the passion you have for doing what you do, and part of that fun is displaying and sharing humor with your clients.

#204 Business Golf
Golf is a great way to develop more personal relationships in business. Chances are, if you play a lot of business golf you'll play with a wide range of players, from very good to very bad. It is important for you to have at least a basic knowledge of the game and its etiquette before combining golf and business.

Every course has a golf professional. Take a couple of lessons to go over the basics of setting up and hitting the variety of shots you will try during a round. Buy golf magazines, which always have mini lessons that help any game. And most importantly, learn the basics of golf etiquette. Golf is a game that places more importance on etiquette than almost any other game, and you can look very bad if you don't follow these rules. Good golfers have more tolerance for bad golfers as long as the bad golfers obey the rules of etiquette and play reasonably quickly.

Finally, from a social standpoint, be careful not to drink too much before or after playing. Remember that you're with business associates. Have fun, but fun while under control.

#205 Sending Thank You Notes
After meetings, especially initial meetings, it's both polite and good business to send a thank you note, thanking the person or people you met with for their time and letting them know how much you look forward to doing business with them.

Thank you notes are best sent hand written, showing that you spent personal time expressing your appreciation. Thank you e-mails are ok, though not as personal or effective. It doesn't take much, either. A short, simple note works best, and puts you in a different light, with more of a personal relationship.

#206 Handling Rejection from Prospective Customers
Without a doubt, there will be times during your entrepreneurial life that you will face being rejected by prospective customers. How you handle this rejection will determine your opportunity for success.

When a prospective client rejects your offer, learn from their objection. This is valuable information that will tell you more about the motivating factors of your customer base. When a client rejects you, they're giving you the reason for not wanting to buy. This can help you enormously when reevaluating your services, products, and business philosophy.

It's also important to remember that more often than not, a rejected offer is really a request for more information. For example, let's suppose you offered a new vacuum cleaner to a prospective client. If it was rejected because the client needed a vacuum cleaner with hypoallergenic filter bags that could be viewed as an opportunity to answer their rejection with a solution and indicate that the product *has* this feature. Or it could be viewed as an opportunity to grow the product line and add this feature to future products.

Networking

None of us has gotten where we are solely by pulling ourselves up from our own bootstraps. We got here because somebody… bent down and helped us.
Thurgood Marshall

#207 The Art of Rubbing Elbows/Networking

There is absolutely an art to rubbing elbows – to networking effectively and with style. Some people think that others are natural at networking, and to a certain extent, that may be true. People with outgoing personalities many times fair better in networking situations because that's who they are, they're used to being around people, and they're used to conversing. There are specific things, though, that make them and others more effective at rubbing elbows.

Most importantly, always be on your best behavior. Your best behavior can involve several factors, including:

- Dress appropriately for the event or occasion.

- Demonstrate proper etiquette in terms of shaking hands and introducing others.

- Don't drink alcohol, or at least keep it to a minimum.

- Be careful what you say. Personal comments or opinions may be inappropriate. Particularly when talking with someone for the first time, stick with topics related to the event or each other's lines of business.

- Look at the person with whom you're talking. Don't let your eyes stray to see who else is at the event. Focus on the conversation you're having at the time.

When attending a networking event, go with an idea of what you'd like to accomplish, such as meeting new faces, or meeting up with someone you planned to meet. Don't attend only to be seen. If there is good accomplished from that, it will happen as a byproduct of going with a purpose in mind.

#208 Networking that Creates Leads
When you're networking, whether it's at a Chamber of Commerce breakfast, conference, Rotary International meetings, or anywhere else, the key that creates leads is to be both memorable and specific. Be memorable through how you introduce yourself – who you are, what you do, where you work, etc. Be specific by having a good explanation of what you do and how it helps people.

Also, when networking, don't spend too much time with any one person. Remember your goal – to network. You need to meet people to generate the beginnings of relationships that could lead to work. You can always follow up a meeting with a lunch or another meeting if you want to spend more time with anyone in particular. Networking involves reaching out to many people – as many as you can.

Finally, follow up. When you make contact with someone, follow up, especially if you said you would. Your follow-up is the next key step after making that initial contact. If you follow up in a timely manner and you were memorable when you met, the relationship has begun, and your chance of business with that person, if synergy exists, has increased significantly.

#209 Using Your Network for Networking
Carry business cards with you all day, every day. Consider giving two to each individual so that they can help you to network by passing along the extra card.

Another way to use your network for networking is to establish partnerships with companies who can add to your service or product offering without competing with your business. For example, if you operate a bakery consider partnering with a party supply store. If you are a financial consultant, consider partnering with other business consulting groups who can offer advice to your clients on other topics such as marketing, sales, human resources, or risk management. Partnering with these companies can help you fill your clients' needs without adding expenses and overhead to your own company and will ensure greater follow-on business.

In addition to partnering with like businesses, you can also consider sharing customer information with your partners. Many like businesses will provide you with customer databases for direct mailing purposes in return for the same from you. This can be a valuable resource as it's typically a current and qualified list of people who are interested in services and products similar to those you offer.

#210 Benefit from Affiliate Programs

As a business owner, you can't be everything to everyone. But you can direct customers to businesses who do offer a solution to their need. On the Internet, this kind of referral process is often called an affiliate program.

If your business has a web site, you could benefit financially through providing a link to other web sites that offer services or products that you don't. For example, PayPal®, Amazon®, and Barnes & Noble, Inc. offer you the ability to profit through link referrals to their products. If a consumer makes a purchase as a result of clicking through from a link on your web site and you've signed up for the affiliate program you reap a percentage of that sale.

Conducting a search for "Affiliate Programs" on any major search engine such as Yahoo.com or Google.com will result in a number of directories that list opportunities for you to participate.

You can also design your own affiliate program and increase consumer awareness and sales. Offer affiliates a percentage of sales that result from customers coming to your site through clicking on a link on their site. This is a great way to market through creating a virtual sales team.

171

#211 Forming Strategic Alliances
Good strategic alliances can be a very powerful tool to companies, particularly small companies. When you're small and trying to be or appear large, strategic alliances can help to expand your team without expanding your overhead.

The best alliances create a mutually beneficial relationship for you and the individual or company with which you have the alliance. By strategy, the emphasis is on forming alliances that fit the overall direction and strategic plan for your company – someone that enhances your abilities to reach your short- and long-term goals.

Strategic alliances help you to avoid adding permanent payroll, including benefits and payroll taxes, to your expenses. You can add resources for a project and not have to carry them beyond that project. You can hand pick expertise that fits the job at hand, specific for that project only.

Regardless of how well you know the individual or company with which you want to form an alliance, have a formal agreement between you and them, defining the relationship as well as possible, complete with a term (length) for the agreement.

Strategic alliances can provide power to your proposals and expertise to your team, helping you to answer the call on jobs you may not have otherwise attempted on your own.

#212 Increasing Business through Distributors
You're a small company with a good product. You are confident that the product can sell, but you don't have the financial resources to hire a team of fifty salespeople to market and sell the product for you. You also don't have the staff resources to support those that purchase the product. How do you make your good idea and good product create success for you?

Distributors can help market, sell, and support your product. Understand that you'll give up a piece of the pie, probably in the form of a percentage of revenue generated from sales, to have distributors support you. Some of the pros and cons of using distributors include:

Pros

- If you hire a distributor already in your market, they know how to sell in that market because they will have presumably already been doing so.

- Because they have been selling in your market, they have resources established specific to effectively market and sell what you have.

- You don't have to incur the payroll and overhead expenses of bringing on these skills to your payroll.

- If the relationship doesn't work, you can cut it off quickly, as long as your agreement allows.

Cons

- Nobody knows your business or your product like you do, including a distributor.

- You could be only one of many things the distributor is distributing.

- Distributors may care most about the biggest fish — who will generate the most sales and profit.

- Communication with the distributor is rarely daily like it is with an employee.

Pros and cons are almost evenly distributed. The weight of each is dependent on the type of business you have and how willing or well you are able to manage the drawbacks. Distributors can and in many cases do work extremely well.

#213 Networking with Your Local Chamber
Local Chambers of Commerce are typically county or city central points of contact and activity for businesses. Some Chambers have very active membership and participation in events, from breakfasts featuring speakers to after-hour networking opportunities. Networking with your local Chamber can mean contacts in your area that will help your business grow, whether it's through gaining clients or strategic partners.

Chambers also offer advertising opportunities through Chamber newsletters or web sites. Active Chamber membership uses these resources to keep up with what's happening, and through advertising, you would be seen.

Networking involves meeting people and getting your name out, and your Chamber of Commerce offers opportunities to do both through sponsored events and advertising. Joining your local Chamber is a small investment, particularly if you're active and make use of your membership.

#214 Give a Speech or Volunteer for a Career Day at School
Giving a speech or volunteering for a career day at a local school can be a very rewarding experience, both in terms of doing something good in your community and in being able to practice telling people what you do and how you do it.

There are times when you get so close to what you do that you don't know how to explain it, particularly in laymen's terms so that everyone can understand it. When you present at a school, you immediately know that your audience probably won't understand what you do unless you explain it clearly and simply. It's a technique that should be carried over to everyone – explain things simply and clearly. Let questions dictate how much more detail people want to know.

Being involved in speaking or volunteering at schools is rewarding because you see why you do what you do. You realize that the youngsters you're talking to are the same ones that will be leading in the not-too-distant future. Their questions are usually not sugar coated and come from a refreshing and honest angle. Speaking or volunteering in a school once a year helps you to keep your perspective.

#215 Conversation Topics to Avoid
Dressing conservatively, whether it's business formal or casual, is the safe way to go. It won't alienate others. Likewise, be particular about the types of topics to choose to discuss in business, whether you're on or off duty, so to speak.

There are the obvious choices to avoid: politics and religion. Also be careful when making jokes, particularly if they have a sexist or ethnic slant to them. Be careful when poking fun at someone. Know whether they can take the abuse or not. Sometimes self-deprecating humor is best. Likewise, use caution when talking about other individuals within your or their company, or even competitors.

It's important to develop relationships, but it doesn't need to happen overnight. Tread lightly while getting to know the person. Use good judgment when choosing what to discuss, and when possible, particularly early in your relationship, let them take the lead. You will learn best what topics to discuss by hearing what topics they enjoy discussing.

#216 Attend a Trade Show or Conference
One of the greatest ways to network is through attending trade shows and conferences. You don't have to be an exhibitor to make networking connections. Just be sure to bring your business cards and an outgoing personality!

If you're unaware of any upcoming trade shows or conferences, look for advertisements in magazines related to your industry or contact your local economic development corporation. .

You can also search for events using the following resources:

> *Trade show Week Data Book* – a comprehensive directory of nearly 5,000 trade shows and consumer expositions.
>
> *TSNN.com* – a web site dedicated to promoting trade shows and other events for businesses.
>
> *Go-events.com* – leading search engine for global business events.

Remember you can't just show up and expect to make new business contacts. You'll need to attend the receptions and make an effort to introduce yourself to other attendees who are interested in networking as well.

Sales

One of the best ways to persuade others is with your ears – by listening to them.
Dean Rusk

#217 Five Selling Strategies

1. Provide a value add to the customer without adding cost by making him/her feel good about the purchase.

2. Become indispensable to your clients to encourage repeat business and loyalty.

3. Exposure. Exposure. Exposure. Reach out and get in the faces of prospective customers and leave an imprint wherever you go.

4. Network, partner, and collaborate. If you can't beat them, join them.

5. Do it differently. If you're not getting the results you want from your selling strategies, try something new. Differentiate yourself from your old ways and the ways of your competition.

#218 Writing an Effective Sales Letter

Your goal needs to be to first have your letter read particularly if you are writing to someone you don't know. After that, once your letter is read, it needs to be persuasive. The last thing you want is for your letter to come across as junk – something the reader won't read and will file under "t" for trash.

First things first, make your letter personal. It needs to be addressed to an individual. Think of it as a letter to a friend while maintaining standards in writing letters, such as:

January 13, 2012

Mr. John Q. Public
President
The Public Group
1001 West Main Street
Springfield, NY 10101

Dear John,

Depending on your industry or how you want to present yourself, you may want to be more formal and say "Dear Mr. Public" instead. The personalization of a letter, and even the envelope on which it arrives, is critical to having the letter opened and read.

End each letter with a salutation, your name, title, and a personal, real signature, so that they know you took the time to sign it yourself. For example:

Regards,

(With enough room to fit your signature)

Jane Doe
Director
The Learning Institute

Finally, once you've maximized the chances of having your letter read and you have covered your bases with regard to addressing the letter and finishing it, focus on the content.

A good rule of thumb for the content of a letter is to:

- Identify the purpose of your letter up front.
- Cover your points thoroughly.
- Restate your points as they relate to the purpose.

In other words, (1) tell them what you want to say, (2) say it, and (3) say what you just said. Repetition translates to retention – people retain what they hear more than once. By covering all of these steps, you will maximize the chances that your letter will be both read and understood.

#219 Survive During Tough Times
The economy and your market changes, and during downtimes, it may be a challenge just to survive. Surviving

during tough times can make you much stronger – leaner and meaner, if you will – by streamlining and focusing your business even more. Your streamlining may be for purely survival purposes at the time, but will benefit your business in the long run as well.

There are several important things you can do to increase your chances of survival during tough times, including:

- Reduce your expenses. Take a critical look at your company, from payroll to office supplies, and see where you can control or reduce your expenses. It may require tough decisions like layoffs, but when it comes to survival, you have to do tough things, which may include cutting staff.

- Refinance your debt. If you have a good banking relationship, you may be able to take your debt and consolidate it at more affordable rates, helping to reduce your monthly expenses.

- Retain key staff. If you can avoid staff reductions in key staff, it can help you to stay on course with your clients or products, helping the company to maintain excellence despite cuts. Turnover can be costly, particularly when losing key employees with critical knowledge or relationships.

- Don't lose focus on your customers. The worst thing you can do is to fail to provide the best support possible for your customers. They made you. Don't lose that perspective. Without them, you don't exist. Even in tough times, maintaining that focus is critical.

#220 Bid Successfully on Government Contracts
Government contracts can be very helpful in making your business successful. Many businesses survive solely on government contracts. Knowing how to compete for

government jobs is critical, otherwise you will be wasting your time.

Government procurements always have very specific rules for the format and submission of your bid. You must obey every rule, crossing every "t" and dotting every "i," to have any chance of being considered in this very competitive environment.

Attend the pre-bid meeting, if there is one. Follow every rule defined in the Request for Proposal (RFP). Submit your bid as specified by the RFP, with the correct number of copies and on time. These simple things will at least give you a fighting chance.

#221 Establish a Referral Program
One of the easiest and best ways to get the word out about your company's services or products is to establish a referral program. Ask your colleagues, partners, friends, and family to refer prospective clients to your business and offer them a percentage of any sales that result from their referral. You'll need to determine how much each client is worth to you and what you're willing to offer for the referral.

One thing to consider when establishing a referral program is whether you're going to pay a one-time referral reward or a percentage of all future business the referred client brings you. You may even decide to put a cap on the referral reward and limit it to the first year's sales or first sale only. Regardless of whatever terms you come up with for your referral plan, be consistent with those who refer clients to you and have a specific program in mind before explaining it to others.

If you can't afford to offer a percentage of sale(s) to people who refer clients to you offer a simple gesture of thanks and send them tickets to an event, a thank you card, or take them out for lunch to show your appreciation.

#222 Finding a Good Salesperson
In a small or start-up business, the founder of the business is typically the main, and sometimes only, salesperson. One of the challenging parts of expanding your business is bringing another salesperson on that shares the founder's conviction, knowledge, morals, and message.

One of the necessary elements, knowledge, can be obtained by looking within your industry. Find a salesperson with direct experience within your industry or a like industry. That person may have much of the same knowledge and message that you do. From there, it's up to you as head of your company to instill everything about your company – what you do, how you do it, the passion with which you do it, etc. – into your salespeople.

Also, think about how your prospective salesperson will present your company. How is their appearance? Are they well spoken? Can they handle technology? Do they have a broad base of knowledge beyond what they're selling? Are they relationship builders? These elements make for well-rounded salespeople.

In summary, the short list of things you may look for in a good salesperson includes:

- Knowledge of industry.
- Ability to communicate message.
- Business ethics.
- Appearance.
- Knowledge beyond industry.
- Ability to develop and retain relationships.

#223 Always Provide a Little More Value than Your Customer Expects
Satisfying your customers' expectations isn't good enough these days. If you want to increase your chances of getting repeat business, give your customers *more* than they expect.

On that note we end with one final way to entrepreneurial success . . .

Tools for Effective Sales

Being truly effective at selling to a wide range of potential clients is more than being a nice person or knowing the right people. To be effective to the masses, an effective salesperson has a wide range of tools at their disposal to increase their chances at sales.

Know your audience. By knowing your audience, you will know which tools to use for particular sales, customizing your message to best meet the needs of those to whom you're trying to sell. A list of potential tools to use to increase your sales effectiveness includes:

- Good writing ability to communicate initial ideas through e-mail or letter.

- Good phone skills to communicate initial thoughts via conversation.

- Professional business cards.

- Literature or other handouts that portray professionalism and a specific message.

- Professional web site to which to point people for more information.

- High quality presentation, whether in Microsoft® PowerPoint® or on paper.

Finally, know how to use your network to find answers. There will be times that you're asked questions to which you don't know the answer. Rather than guess or make something up, admit that you don't know the answer, but know how to get it. Your prospects will appreciate your honesty as well as your ability to follow through. Your network is as useful a tool as any.

Recommended Resources

Collins, Jim (2001). *Good to Great.* HarperCollins Publishers Inc.

Godin, Seth (2003). *Purple Cow: Transform Your Business by Being Remarkable.* Portfolio.

Levinson, Jay Conrad (2002). *Guerrilla Publicity: Hundreds of Sure-Fire Tactics to Get Maximum Sales for Minimum Dollars.* Adams Media Corporation.

Mackay, Harvey (1996). *Swim with the Sharks Without Being Eaten Alive: Outsell, Outmanage, Outmotivate, and Outnegotiate Your Competition.* Ballantine Books.

Moltz, Barry (2002). *You Need to Be a Little Crazy: The Truth About Starting and Growing Your Business.* Dearborn Trade Publishing.

Pachter Barbara, and Brody, Marjorie with Anderson, Betsy (1994). *Complete Business Etiquette Handbook.* Prentice Hall Press.

Silber, Lee (1998). *Time Management for the Creative Person: Right-Brain Strategies for Stopping Procrastination, Getting Control of the Clock and Calendar, and Freeing Up Your Time and Your Life.* Three Rivers Press.

Glossary

Accrual basis. A method of accounting in which each item is entered as it is earned or incurred regardless of when actual payments are received or made.

Advisory committee. A corporate support committee formed up of experts in your field that focus on the scientific, technological, engineering, or other aspects of your company.

Angel investors. Individuals, rather than companies or institutions, that provide financing. More often than not, angel investors help fund early-stage companies.

Asset liquidation. Conversion of assets into cash, typically through direct sale.

Banner ad. Term given to most of the advertisements you typically find on web sites. More often than not, the advertiser is paying the owner of those web sites to display that banner.

Benchmarking. A standard by which something can be measured or judged.

Better Business Bureau (BBB). Provides reports on over two million organizations. Consumers often use these reports to investigate organizations prior to doing business or investing.

Bulk mail. Mail consisting of large numbers of identical items (circulars or advertisements) sent to individual addresses at less than first-class rates.

Cash basis. A method of accounting in which each item is entered as payments are received or made.

Certified Financial Planner (CFP). The best-known financial planning designation, given to qualifying planners by the CFP Board of Standards.

Certified Public Accountant (CPA). A special designation given to an accountant who has passed a national uniform examination and has met other requirements. CPA certificates are issued and monitored by state boards of accountancy or similar agencies.

Certified Valuation Analyst (CVA). The CVA accreditation is a statement to the business, professional and legal community that an individual has attained a level of knowledge in business valuations that the National Association of Certified Valuation Analysts (NACVA) considers exemplary and worthy of recognition by awarding the designation of Certified Valuation Analyst (CVA).

Debt financing. Involves securing a bank loan with collateral, such as personal assets, including personal property.

Direct mail. Advertising circulars or other printed matter sent directly through the mail to prospective customers or contributors.

Dun & Bradstreet (D&B). A leading provider of business information used by customers who want to make purchasing decisions with confidence.

E-commerce. Commerce transacted electronically, typically over the Internet.

Employer Identification Number (EIN). Issued by the Federal Government and used to identify your business. Can also include Federal (FEIN) in the name.

Equity financing. Giving up a piece of your company in exchange for financing that will help you to explore more explosive growth options. Equity financing is simply trading money for stock.

Exit strategy. There are three predominant types of exit strategies. You can sell your company, being acquired by someone else. You can attempt to set your company up for an Initial Public Offering (IPO), also called, "going public." You can also be part of a management buyout, where the management team buys parts of the company that they don't already own.

Fixed-asset loans. Long-term, fixed-rate financing to be used for significant fixed assets such as purchasing corporate real estate or expanding existing facilities.

Global Trade Item Number (GTIN). Used to track sales and product orders by retail businesses internationally.

Guerilla marketing. The use of unconventional methods to make sales, including low-cost solutions to address marketing efforts and needs.

Incubators. Business incubators house multiple early-stage businesses and offer shared services and reduced rents. Some incubators provide access to low-cost legal, marketing, and other business services.

Initial Public Offering (IPO). The sale of no less than 25% of the company's equity in the form of common stock or shares through an investment banking firm.

Internal Revenue Service (IRS). The nation's tax collection agency and administers the Internal Revenue Code enacted by Congress.

Limited Liability Corporation (LLC). The most modern of company forms, the LLC is quickly becoming the most popular business entity due to its many benefits over other business structures. Like general corporations, LLCs enjoy the benefits of limited liability along with the advantages of a wide array of business expense deductions and other tax benefits. What may be the main advantage of the LLC is that unlike a general corporation, there is no double taxation.

Meme. Similar to a slogan, a marketing meme is simple, viral in how it spreads, a memorable.

Newsgroups. An area on a computer network, especially the Internet, devoted to the discussion of a specified topic

Payables. Requiring payment on a certain date.

Point of Sale (POS) system. A location where credit card transactions are performed. The card is read magnetically, and the cardholder's signature is obtained as insurance against the transaction. This is the most secure form of credit card commerce.

Press kit. A complete package that supports your press release and provides the editor with additional information from which they can build a complete story.

Receivables. Business assets due to one business from another.

Request for Proposal (RFP). Announcements that specify a topic of research, methods to be used, product to be delivered, and appropriate applicants sought. Proposals submitted in response to RFPs generally result in the award of a contract. Also can be Request for Quotation (RFQ), typically requesting quotation without as much accompanying material.

Service Corps of Retired Executives (SCORE). A nonprofit association dedicated to providing entrepreneurs with free, confidential face-to-face and email business counseling. Business counseling and workshops are offered at chapter offices across the country.

Small Business Administration (SBA). Federal government agency that administers loan guarantee and related small business development programs

Stock options. Widely used by companies to both reward employees and/or Board members and to secure key staff so that critical turnover is avoided. In most cases, people are given stock options in the form of convertible shares at a certain price, presumably later convertible at that low price into real stock. Stock options usually have a "shelf life" of three, five, or ten years, and are sometimes given to employees in stages.

SWOT analysis. Strengths, weaknesses, opportunities, and threats - a tool used for auditing an organization and its environment and helps you focus on key marketing issues

Universal Product Code (UPC). Twelve digit bar codes used to identify products and information about your business. Some bar code numbers may be shortened if there are four consecutive zeros in the number, in which case they may be removed

Venture Capital (VC) firms. Typically invest larger amounts but require a larger equity share in the company in which they are investing. They also typically require a seat or more on the company's Board of Directors.

Index

D

E

Expenses · 38, 39, 81, 109, 180

F

Failure · 54, 86
Faxes · 159
Financial Projections · 31
Financing · 26, 31, 58
Firing · 77, 78
Fiscal Tax Year · 36
Forecasts · 59, 109
Fraud · 40
Freebies · 4, 105, 106, 117, 131
Funding · 26

G

Global Traide Item Number · 21
Goals · 59
Golf · 166
Guerrilla Marketing · 106

H

Handshake · 163
Hiring · 62, 67, 71, 72, 73, 123, 182
Hotels · 91

I

Incorporating · 8
Incubator · 27
Initial Public Offering · 27, 43
Insurance · 61
Intern · 71
Internal Revenue Service · 41, 52
Internet Marketing · 143, 144, 146, 147, 150, 153, 157, 158
Interview · 62, 65, 72
Intranet · 156
Introductions · 162, 163
Investors · 31

O

P

R

S

T

U

V

W

About the Authors

Brendan McGinty is President & CEO of Leo Media, Inc. He has over 20 years of experience in corporate management and has helped many companies form and mature. Brendan is also President & CEO of Campaign Advisory Corporation, a political consulting firm, and Managing Director of HMM Development LLC, a real estate management firm. He was previously Vice President of NovaNET Learning, Inc. (now Pearson Education), a leading provider of on-line education. Brendan was featured in the 2003 edition of Fundamentals of Management (Pearson-Prentice Hall), has lectured on entrepreneurship at the University of Illinois, and was a finalist for the Illinois High Tech Award.

Sherry Schuller is Vice President of Leo Media, Inc. She is the founder of the Conference on Strategic Growth for Businesses and Entrepreneurs. Sherry has assisted many organizations with strategic planning, branding, marketing, advertising design, training, and application development. She was previously an Internet Specialist for IBM's leading North American distributor, Business Partner Solutions (now Avnet), and an independent consultant for various firms, including PRIMEDIA, Inc., the leading provider of targeted content and integrated marketing solutions in consumer and business-to-business sectors.

About Leo Media

Founded in 1994, Leo Media, Inc. is a business growth consulting firm based in Savoy, Illinois, near the University of Illinois at Urbana-Champaign. Leo's services include custom e-learning design and development, marketing & advertising, and business advisory for organizations worldwide.

For more information about Leo Media, visit http://www.leomedia.net.

For additional entrepreneurial strategies, visit http://www.leostrategies.com.